Narrative of the Life of

Frederick Douglass
An American Slave

THE EXCHANGE

**What is an
education
worth?**

Narrative of the Life of
Frederick Douglass
An American Slave

by FREDERICK DOUGLASS

 HAMPTON-BROWN

Narrative of the Life of Frederick Douglass, An American Slave by Frederick Douglass.

Front cover portrait of Frederick Douglass © by Getty Images.
Back cover North Star, June 2, 1849—Library of Congress Serial and Government Publication Division.
Map on p. 10 by Mapping Specialists, Ltd.

On-Page Coach™ (introductions, questions, on-page glossaries), The Exchange,
back cover summary, cover design © Hampton-Brown.

Hampton-Brown
P.O. Box 223220
Carmel, California 93922
800-333-3510
www.hampton-brown.com

Printed in the United States of America

ISBN-13: 978-0-7362-3164-0
ISBN-10: 0-7362-3164-1

12 13 14 15 10 9 8 7 6

TABLE OF CONTENTS

INTRODUCTION

The *Narrative* of the Life of Frederick Douglass is about one man's journey from slavery to freedom. Douglass writes about growing up as a slave in the early 1800s on a farm in Baltimore, Maryland. Life for a slave was brutal. Douglass was treated like an animal until he escaped to the North in 1838. He and his relatives were beaten and whipped by their masters many times.

Douglass tells of the moment he understood why he and others were enslaved. He realized that not only the slave owner, but a lack of education, kept them in slavery. That is why, for Douglass, **literacy** was the key to being free. However, the slave owners did not want African Americans to learn to read and write. They felt that literacy would give slaves too much power. An educated slave would not tolerate the horrible

Key Concepts

narrative *n.* story that describes a sequence of events

literacy *n.* the ability to read and write

discrimination that characterized slavery.

Frederick Douglass was an example of this. He taught himself to read and write. Then he was able to learn about the work **abolitionists** were doing in the North to end slavery. He was also able to write the story of his life.

The abolition movement became stronger in the 1830s under the leadership of William Lloyd Garrison. Garrison's newsletter, the *Liberator*, first published in 1831, spoke strongly against slavery. Garrison's message grew stronger as the leaders Lucretia Mott, Wendell Phillips, Charles Sumner, and Gerrit Smith also spoke out against slavery. Believing that slavery was morally wrong, these people and others like them fought to end it. Acting on their beliefs, they helped many slaves escape to the North. The most famous escape path was the Underground Railroad. The Underground Railroad was a network of people that hid slaves and helped them travel from slave states to free states. The most famous conductor of this railroad was Harriet Tubman. This former slave secretly guided many runaways out of Maryland.

Key Concepts

discrimination *n.* unfair treatment of a person or a group

abolitionist *n.* person who fought for the end of slavery during the 18th and 19th centuries

Though born into slavery, Frederick Douglass later became a counsel to four presidents. He also served as United States Minister to Haiti. Although lacking formal education, Douglass became a well-known and respected **orator**. He spoke at universities around the world, promoting his message of freedom and the power within the human spirit to break the chains of slavery.

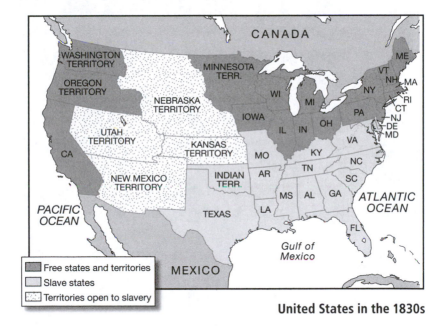

United States in the 1830s

Key Concepts

orator *n.* person who gives public speeches

CHAPTER I

I was born in Tuckahoe, near Hillsborough, about twelve miles from Easton, in Talbot County, Maryland. I have no accurate knowledge of my age, never having seen any authentic record containing it. By far the larger part of the slaves know as little of their ages as horses know of theirs. It is the wish of most masters within my knowledge to keep their slaves **thus ignorant**. I do not remember ever meeting a slave who could tell of his birthday. They seldom come nearer to it than planting-time, harvest-time, cherry-time, spring-time, or fall-time. Not knowing my own was a source of unhappiness to me even during childhood. The white children could tell their ages. I could not tell why I **ought to be deprived of the same privilege**. I was not allowed to **make any inquiries of** my master concerning it. He deemed all such inquiries on the part of a slave **improper and impertinent**, and evidence of a restless spirit. The nearest estimate I can give makes

....

thus ignorant not knowing their ages

ought to be deprived of the same privilege was not allowed to know my age

make any inquiries of ask

improper and impertinent wrong and rude

me now between twenty-seven and twenty-eight years old. I learned this from hearing my master say, some time during 1835, I was about seventeen years old.

My mother was named Harriet Bailey. She was the daughter of Isaac and Betsey Bailey, both colored, and quite dark. My mother **was of a darker complexion** than either my grandmother or grandfather.

My father was a white man. He was **admitted to be such** by all I ever heard speak of my parentage. The opinion was also whispered that my master was my father; but I don't know if this is true. The means of knowing was withheld from me. My mother and I were separated when I was but an infant—before I knew her as my mother. It is a common custom, in the part of Maryland from which I ran away, to separate children from their mothers at a very early age. Frequently, before the child has reached its twelfth month, its mother is taken from it, and **hired out on some** farm a considerable distance off. The child is placed under the care of an old woman, too old for field labor. Why this separation is done, I do not know, unless it be to **hinder** the development of the child's affection toward its

···

was of a darker complexion had darker skin
admitted to be such considered white
hired out on some sent out to work on a different
hinder stop

mother, and to blunt and destroy the natural affection of the mother for the child. This is **the inevitable** result.

I never saw my mother, to know her as such, more than four or five times in my life; and each of these times was very short in duration, and at night. She was hired by a Mr. Stewart, who lived about twelve miles from my home. She made her journeys to see me in the night, travelling the whole distance on foot, after working all day. **She was a field hand**, and **a whipping is the penalty of not being** in the field at sunrise, unless a slave has special permission from his or her master to the contrary—a permission which they seldom get, and one that gives to him that gives it the proud name of being a kind master. I do not recollect ever seeing my mother by the light of day. She was with me in the night. She would lie down with me, and get me to sleep, but long before I woke up she was gone. Very little communication ever took place between us. Death soon ended what little we could have while she lived, and with it her hardships and suffering. She died when I was about seven years old, on one of my master's farms, near Lee's Mill. I was not allowed to be

....

the inevitable always the

She was a field hand She worked in the fields

a whipping is the penalty of not being workers were beaten as punishment if they were not

present during her illness, at her death, or burial. She was gone long before I knew anything about it. Never having enjoyed, to any considerable extent, her soothing presence, her tender and watchful care, I received the tidings of her death with much the same emotions I should have probably felt at the death of a stranger.

Called thus suddenly away, she left me without the slightest idea of who my father was. The whisper that my master was my father, may or may not be true. Whether it is true or false, the fact remains, in all its glaring odiousness, **that slaveholders have ordained, and by law established, that the children of slave women shall in all cases follow the condition of their mothers**; and this is done too obviously to administer to their own lusts, and make a gratification of their wicked desires profitable as well as pleasurable. By this cunning arrangement, the slaveholder, in cases not a few, sustains to his slaves the double relation of master and father.

I know of such cases; and it is worthy of remark that such slaves invariably suffer greater hardships, and have more to contend with, than others. They are, in the first

....

that slaveholders have ordained, and by law established, that the children of slave women shall in all cases follow the condition of their mothers that masters have made laws that slave women will always be used to make babies

place, a constant offense to their mistress. She always finds fault with them; they can seldom do anything to please her; she is never better pleased than when she sees them **under the lash**, especially when she suspects her husband of showing to his **mulatto** children favors which he withholds from his black slaves. The master is frequently compelled to sell this class of his slaves, out of **deference** to the feelings of his white wife. As cruel as the deed may strike anyone to be, for a man to sell his own children to human flesh-mongers, it is often the dictate of humanity for him to do so; for, unless he does this, he must not only whip them himself, but must stand by and see one white son tie up his brother, of but few shades darker complexion than himself, and ply the gory lash to his naked back; and if he lisp one word of disapproval, it is **set down to** his parental partiality, and only makes a bad matter worse, both for himself and the slave whom he would protect and defend.

I have had two masters. My first master's name was Anthony. I do not remember his first name. He was generally called Captain Anthony—a title which, I presume, he acquired by sailing a craft on

....

under the lash being beaten; being whipped
mulatto mixed-race, half-white
deference respect
set down to blamed on

the Chesapeake Bay. He was not considered a rich slaveholder. He owned two or three farms and about thirty slaves. His farms and slaves were under the care of **an overseer**. The overseer's name was Plummer. Mr. Plummer was a miserable drunkard, a profane swearer, and a savage monster. He always **went armed with a cowskin and a heavy cudgel**. I have known him to cut and slash the women's heads so horribly, that even master would be enraged at his cruelty, and would threaten to whip him if he did not **mind himself**. Master, however, was not a humane slaveholder. It required extraordinary barbarity on the part of an overseer to affect him. He was a cruel man, hardened by a long life of slaveholding. He would at times seem to take great pleasure in whipping a slave. I have often been awakened at the dawn of day by the most heart-rending shrieks of an own aunt of mine, whom he used to tie **up to a joist**, and whip upon her naked back till she was literally covered with blood. No words, no tears, no prayers from his gory victim, seemed to move his iron heart from its bloody purpose. The louder she screamed, the harder he whipped; and where the blood

....

an overseer a person paid to take care of the farm

went armed with a cowskin and a heavy cudgel carried a whip and club to beat people

mind himself stop being so cruel and violent

up to a joist to a board on the ceiling by the hands

ran fastest, there he whipped longest. He would whip her to make her scream, and whip her to make her hush. Not until he was overcome by fatigue, would he cease to swing the blood-clotted cowskin. I remember the first time I ever witnessed this horrible exhibition. I was quite a child, but I well remember it. I never shall forget it **whilst I remember anything**. It was the first of a long series of such outrages, of which I was doomed to be a witness and a participant. It struck me with awful force. It was the blood-stained gate, the entrance to the hell of slavery, through which I was about to pass. It was a most terrible spectacle. I wish I could **commit to paper** the feelings with which I beheld it.

This occurrence took place very soon after I went to live with my old master and under the following circumstances. Aunt Hester went out one night—where or for what I do not know—and happened to be absent when my master desired her presence. He had ordered her not to go out evenings, and warned her that she must never let him catch her in company with a young man, who was paying attention to her belonging to Colonel Lloyd. The young man's name

....

whilst I remember anything for the rest of my life
commit to paper write about

was Ned Roberts, generally called Lloyd's Ned. Why master was so careful of her, may be **safely left to conjecture**. She was a woman of noble form, and of graceful proportions, having very few equals, and fewer superiors, in personal appearance, among the colored or white women of our neighborhood.

Aunt Hester had not only disobeyed his orders in going out, but had been found in company with Lloyd's Ned. I found out, from what he said while whipping her, that this was the **chief offense**. Had he been a man of pure morals himself, he might have been thought interested in protecting the innocence of my aunt; but those who knew him will not suspect him of any such virtue. Before he **commenced** whipping Aunt Hester, he took her into the kitchen, and stripped her from neck to waist, leaving her neck, shoulders, and back, entirely naked. He then told her to cross her hands, calling her at the same time a d—d b—h. After crossing her hands, he tied them with a strong rope, and led her to a stool under a large hook in the joist, put in for the purpose. He made her get upon the stool, and tied her hands to the hook. She now stood **fair** for his infernal

....

safely left to conjecture because of her beauty
chief offense worst thing she had done wrong
commenced began
fair naked

purpose. Her arms were stretched up at their full length, so that she stood on the ends of her toes. He then said to her, "Now, you d—d b—h, I'll **learn you how to** disobey my orders!" and after rolling up his sleeves, he commenced to **lay on** the heavy cowskin, and soon the warm, red blood (amid heartrending shrieks from her, and horrid oaths from him) came dripping to the floor. I was so terrified and horror-stricken at the sight, that I hid myself in a closet, and dared not venture out till long after the **bloody transaction** was over. I expected it would be my turn next. It was all new to me. I had never seen anything like it before. I had always lived with my grandmother **on the outskirts** of the plantation, where she was put to raise the children of the younger women. I had therefore been, until now, out of the way of the bloody scenes that often occurred on the plantation.

....

learn you how to teach you what happens when you

lay on whip her with

bloody transaction whipping

on the outskirts on the far end

BEFORE YOU MOVE ON...

1. **Narrator** Reread page 13. Who tells the story? Describe the narrator.

2. **Conclusions** Reread page 16. How was a slaveholder sometimes "master and father"?

LOOK AHEAD Read Chapter 2 to see where Frederick lived as a slave.

CHAPTER II

My master's family consisted of two sons, Andrew and Richard; one daughter, Lucretia, and her husband, Captain Thomas Auld. They lived in one house, on the home plantation of Colonel Edward Lloyd. My master was Colonel Lloyd's clerk and superintendent. He was what might be called the **overseer of the overseers**. I spent two years of childhood on this plantation in my old master's family. It was here that I witnessed the bloody transaction recorded in the first chapter; and as I received my first impressions of slavery on this plantation, I will give some description of it, and of slavery as it there existed. The plantation is about twelve miles north of Easton, in Talbot County, and is situated on the border of Miles River. The **principal products** raised upon it were tobacco, corn, and wheat. **These were raised in great abundance**; so that, with the products of this and the other farms belonging to him, he was able to keep in almost constant

....

overseer of the overseers head boss

principal products main crops

These were raised in great abundance He grew a lot of these crops

22

employment a **large sloop**, in carrying them to market at Baltimore. This sloop was named Sally Lloyd, in honor of one of the colonel's daughters. My master's son-in-law, Captain Auld, was master of the vessel; **she was otherwise manned** by the colonel's own slaves. Their names were Peter, Isaac, Rich, and Jake. These were **esteemed** very highly by the other slaves, and looked upon as the privileged ones of the plantation; for it was no small affair, in the eyes of the slaves, to be allowed to see Baltimore.

Colonel Lloyd kept from three to four hundred slaves on his home plantation, and owned a large number more on the neighboring farms belonging to him. The names of the farms nearest to the home plantation were Wye Town and New Design. Wye Town was under the overseership of a man named Noah Willis. New Design was under the overseership of a Mr. Townsend. The overseers of these, and all the rest of the farms, numbering over twenty, received advice and direction from the managers of the home plantation. This was the great business place. It was the **seat of government** for the whole twenty farms. All disputes among the

....

large sloop large ship
she was otherwise manned the ship was taken care of
esteemed thought of
seat of government control center

overseers were settled here. If a slave was convicted **of any high misdemeanor, became unmanageable, or evinced a determination** to run away, he was brought immediately here, severely whipped, put on board the sloop, carried to Baltimore, and sold to Austin Woolfolk, or some other slave-trader, as a warning to the slaves remaining.

Here, too, the slaves of all the other farms received their monthly allowance of food, and their yearly clothing. The men and women slaves received, as their monthly allowance of food, eight pounds of pork, or its equivalent in fish, and one bushel of cornmeal. Their yearly clothing consisted of two **coarse** linen shirts, one pair of linen trousers, like the shirts, one jacket, one pair of trousers for winter, made of coarse negro cloth, one pair of stockings, and one pair of shoes; the whole of which could not have cost more than seven dollars. The allowance of the slave children was given to their mothers, or the old women having the care of them. The children unable to work in the field had neither shoes, stockings, jackets, nor trousers, given to them. Their clothing consisted of two coarse linen shirts per

....

of any high misdemeanor, became unmanageable, or evinced a determination of breaking a rule, was difficult to control, or wanted

coarse rough

year. When these failed them, they went naked until the next allowance-day. Children from seven to ten years old, of both sexes, almost naked, might be seen at all seasons of the year.

There were no beds given the slaves, unless one coarse blanket be considered such, and none but the men and women had these. This, however, is not considered **a very great privation**. They find less difficulty from the want of beds, than from the want of time to sleep; for when their day's work in the field is done, most of them having their washing, mending, and cooking to do, and having few or none of the **ordinary facilities** for doing either of these, very many of their sleeping hours are consumed in preparing for the field the coming day; and when this is done, old and young, male and female, married and single, drop down side by side, on one common bed—the cold, damp floor— each covering himself or herself with their miserable blankets; and here they sleep till they are **summoned** to the field by the driver's horn. At the sound of this, all must rise, and be off to the field. There must be no halting; every one must be at his or her post; and

....

a very great privation something they really need
ordinary facilities needed tools
summoned called

woe betides them who don't hear this morning summons to the field; for if they are not awakened by the sense of hearing, they are by the sense of feeling: no age nor sex finds any favor. Mr. Severe, the overseer, used to stand by the door of the quarter, armed with a large hickory stick and heavy cowskin, ready to whip anyone who was so unfortunate as not to hear, or, from any other cause, was prevented from being ready to start for the field at the sound of the horn.

Mr. Severe was rightly named: he was a cruel man. I have seen him whip a woman, causing the blood to run half an hour at the time; and this, too, in the midst of her crying children, pleading for their mother's release. He seemed to take pleasure in **manifesting his fiendish barbarity**. Added to his cruelty, he was a profane swearer. It was enough to **chill the blood and stiffen the hair of** an ordinary man to hear him talk. Scarce a sentence escaped him but that was commenced or concluded by some horrid oath. The field was the place to witness his cruelty and profanity. His presence made it both the field of **blood and of blasphemy**. From the rising till the going down of the sun, he was

....

woe betides them bad things happened to those
manifesting his fiendish barbarity being extremely violent
chill the blood and stiffen the hair of scare
blood and of blasphemy beatings and curses

cursing, raving, cutting, and slashing among the slaves of the field, in the most frightful manner. His career was short. He died very soon after I went to Colonel Lloyd's; and he died as he lived, uttering, with his dying groans, bitter curses and horrid oaths. His death was regarded by the slaves as the result of **a merciful providence**.

Mr. Severe's place was filled by a Mr. Hopkins. He was a very different man. He was less cruel, less profane, and made less noise, than Mr. Severe. His **course was characterized by no extraordinary demonstrations of** cruelty. He whipped, but seemed to take no pleasure in it. He was called by the slaves a good overseer.

The home plantation of Colonel Lloyd looked like a country village. All the mechanical operations for all the farms were performed here. The shoemaking and mending, **the blacksmithing, cartwrighting, coopering**, weaving, and grain-grinding, were all performed by the slaves on the home plantation. The whole place wore a business-like aspect very unlike the neighboring farms. The number of houses, too,

....

a merciful providence good luck

course was characterized by no extraordinary demonstrations of actions did not show extreme

the blacksmithing, cartwrighting, coopering working with metal, making carts, making wooden tubs

conspired to give it advantage over the neighboring farms. It was called by the slaves the *Great House Farm.* Few privileges were esteemed higher, by the slaves of the out-farms, than that of being selected to do errands at the Great House Farm. It was associated in their minds with greatness. A representative could not be prouder of his election to a seat in the American Congress, than a slave on one of the out-farms would be of his election to do errands at the Great House Farm. They regarded it as evidence of **great confidence reposed in them by their overseers**; and it was because of this, as well as a constant desire to be out of the field from under the driver's lash, that they esteemed it a high privilege, one worth careful living for. He was called the smartest and most trusty fellow, who had this honor **conferred upon** him the most frequently. The competitors for this office sought as **diligently** to please their overseers, as the office-seekers in the political parties seek to please and deceive the people. The same traits of character might be seen in Colonel Lloyd's slaves, as are seen in the slaves of the political parties.

The slaves selected to go to the Great House Farm, for

....

great confidence reposed in them by their overseers the masters having a strong trust in their abilities

conferred upon given to

diligently carefully

the monthly allowance for themselves and their fellow-slaves, were peculiarly enthusiastic. While on their way, they would make the dense old woods, for miles around, **reverberate** with their wild songs, revealing at once the highest joy and the deepest sadness. They would compose and sing as they went along, consulting neither time nor tune. The thought that came up, came out—if not in the word, in the sound—and as frequently in the one as in the other. They would sometimes sing the **most pathetic sentiment** in the most **rapturous** tone, and the most rapturous sentiment in the most pathetic tone. Into all of their songs they would manage to sing something about the Great House Farm. They would especially do this when leaving home. They would then sing most exultingly the following words—

"I am going away to the Great House Farm!
O, yea! O, yea! O!"

I did not, when a slave, understand the deep meaning of those rude and apparently incoherent songs. I was myself **within the circle**; so that I neither saw nor heard

....

reverberate shake noisily
most pathetic sentiment saddest thoughts
rapturous joyful
within the circle on the Great House Farm

as those outside the circle might see and hear. They told a tale of woe which was then altogether beyond my **feeble comprehension**; they were tones loud, long, and deep; they breathed the prayer and complaint of souls boiling over with the bitterest anguish. Every tone was a testimony against slavery, and a prayer to God for **deliverance** from chains. The hearing of those wild notes always depressed my spirit, and filled me with ineffable sadness. I have frequently found myself in tears while hearing them. The mere recurrence to those songs, even now, afflicts me; and while I am writing these lines, an expression of feeling has already found its way down my cheek. To those songs I trace my first glimmering conception of the **dehumanizing character** of slavery. I can never get rid of that conception. Those songs still follow me, to deepen my hatred of slavery, and quicken my sympathies for my brethren in bonds. If any one wishes to be impressed with the soul-killing effects of slavery, let him go to Colonel Lloyd's plantation, and, on allowance-day, place himself in the deep pine woods, and there let him, in silence, analyze the sounds that shall pass through the chambers of his soul—and if he is not

....

feeble comprehension little understanding

deliverance freedom

dehumanizing character animal-like cruelty

impressed, it will only be because "there is no **flesh in his obdurate** heart."

I have often been utterly astonished, since I came to the North, to find people who could speak of the singing, among slaves, as evidence of their contentment and happiness. Just the opposite is true. Slaves sing most when they are most unhappy. The songs of the slave represent the sorrows of his heart; and he is relieved by them, only as an aching heart is relieved by its tears. At least, such is my experience. I have often sung to drown my sorrow, but seldom to express my happiness. Crying for joy, and singing for joy, were completely different to me while **in the jaws of slavery**. The singing of a man **cast away upon a desolate** island might be as appropriately considered as evidence of contentment and happiness, as the singing of a slave; the songs of the one and of the other are prompted by the same emotion.

---

flesh in his obdurate feeling in his

in the jaws of slavery trapped as a slave

cast away upon a desolate left alone on an isolated

BEFORE YOU MOVE ON...

1. **Setting** Frederick Douglass lived on a plantation in Maryland. What else can you tell about the setting?

2. **Conclusions** Reread pages 30–31. Why did the songs of slaves fill Frederick with so much sadness?

LOOK AHEAD Did slaves complain about their masters? Read Chapters 3–5 to find out.

CHAPTER III

Colonel Lloyd kept a large and finely cultivated garden, which **afforded almost constant employment for** four men, besides the chief gardener (Mr. M'Durmond). This garden was probably the greatest attraction of the place. During the summer months, people came from far and near—from Baltimore, Easton, and Annapolis—to see it. It **abounded in** fruits of almost every description, from the hardy apple of the North to the delicate orange of the South. This garden was a large source of trouble on the plantation. Its excellent fruit was quite a temptation to the hungry swarms of boys, as well as the older slaves, belonging to the colonel, few of whom could resist it. Scarcely a day passed, during the summer, but that some slave had to take the lash for stealing fruit. The colonel had to **resort to all kinds of stratagems** to keep his slaves out of the garden. The last and most successful one was that of **tarring** his fence all around;

....

afforded almost constant employment for gave work to
abounded in grew many
resort to all kinds of stratagems use different plans
tarring putting a black and sticky liquid on

after which, if a slave was caught with any tar **upon his person**, it was deemed sufficient proof that he had either been into the garden, or had tried to get in. In either case, he was severely whipped by the chief gardener. This plan worked well; the slaves became as fearful of tar as of the lash. They seemed to realize the impossibility of touching tar without being **defiled**.

To describe the wealth of Colonel Lloyd would be like describing the riches of **Job**. He kept from ten to fifteen house-servants. He was said to own a thousand slaves, and I think this estimate quite within the truth. Colonel Lloyd owned so many that he did not know them when he saw them; nor did all the slaves of the out-farms know him. It is reported of him, that, while riding along the road one day, he met a colored man, and addressed him in the usual manner of speaking to colored people on the public highways of the South: "Well, boy, whom do you belong to?" "To Colonel Lloyd," replied the slave. "Well, does the colonel treat you well?" "No, sir," was the ready reply. "What, does he work you too hard?" "Yes, sir." "Well, don't he give you enough to eat?" "Yes, sir, he gives me enough, such

....

upon his person on him
defiled dirtied
Job one of the richest characters in the Bible

as it is."

The colonel, after **ascertaining** where the slave belonged, rode on; the man also went on about his business, not dreaming that he had been **conversing** with his master. He thought, said, and heard nothing more of the matter, until two or three weeks afterwards. The poor man was then informed by his overseer that, for **having found fault with** his master, he was now to be sold to a Georgia trader. He was immediately chained and handcuffed; and thus, without a moment's warning, he was snatched away, and forever **sundered**, from his family and friends, by a hand more unrelenting than death. This is the penalty of telling the truth, of telling the simple truth, in answer to a series of plain questions.

It is partly in consequence of such facts, that slaves, when inquired of as to their condition and the character of their masters, almost universally say they are contented, and that their masters are kind. The slaveholders have been known to send in spies among their slaves, to ascertain their views and feelings in regard to their condition. The frequency of this has

....

ascertaining finding out

conversing talking

having found fault with saying bad things about

sundered separated

caused slaves to establish the **maxim, that a still tongue makes a wise head**. They suppress the truth rather than take the consequences of telling it, and in so doing prove themselves a part of the human family. If they have anything to say of their masters, it is generally in their masters' favor, especially when speaking to **an untried man**. I have been frequently asked, when a slave, if I had a kind master, and do not remember ever to have given a negative answer; nor did I, in pursuing this course, consider myself as uttering what was absolutely false; for I always measured the kindness of my master by the standard of kindness set up among slaveholders around us. Moreover, slaves are like other people, and **imbibe prejudices** quite common to others. They think their own better than that of others. Many, under the influence of this prejudice, think their own masters are better than the masters of other slaves; and this, too, in some cases, when the very reverse is true. Indeed, it is not uncommon for slaves even to fall out and quarrel among themselves about the relative goodness of their masters, each contending for the superior goodness of his own over that of the others.

....

maxim, that a still tongue makes a wise head saying or warning, that a quiet person is a smart person

an untried man a man they do not know

imbibe prejudices share opinions

At the very same time, they **mutually execrate** their masters when viewed separately. It was so on our plantation. When Colonel Lloyd's slaves met the slaves of Jacob Jepson, they seldom parted without a quarrel about their masters; Colonel Lloyd's slaves contending that he was the richest, and Mr. Jepson's slaves that he was the smartest, and most of a man. Colonel Lloyd's slaves would **boast his ability to** buy and sell Jacob Jepson. Mr. Jepson's slaves would boast his ability to whip Colonel Lloyd. These quarrels would almost always end in a fight between **the parties**, and those that whipped were supposed to have **gained the point at issue**. They seemed to think that the greatness of their masters **was transferable to themselves**. It was considered as being bad enough to be a slave; but to be a poor man's slave was deemed a disgrace indeed!

···

mutually execrate both say how evil are
boast his ability to brag how Colonel Lloyd could
the parties the slaves from each plantation
gained the point at issue won
was transferable to themselves made them great, too

CHAPTER IV

Mr. Hopkins remained only a short time in the office of overseer. Why his career was so short, I do not know, but I suppose he **lacked the necessary severity to suit** Colonel Lloyd. Mr. Hopkins was succeeded by Mr. Austin Gore, a man possessing, in an eminent degree, all those traits of character **indispensable** to what is called a first-rate overseer. Mr. Gore had served Colonel Lloyd in the capacity of overseer on one of the out-farms and had shown himself worthy of the high station of overseer at the home or Great House Farm.

Mr. Gore was a **grave** man, and, though a young man, he **indulged in no** jokes, said no funny words, seldom smiled. His words were in perfect keeping with his looks, and his looks were in perfect keeping with his words. Overseers will sometimes indulge in a witty word, even with the slaves; not so with Mr. Gore. He spoke only to command, and commanded only to be

....

lacked the necessary severity to suit was not violent enough to please

indispensable necessary

grave very serious

indulged in no never told

obeyed; he **dealt sparingly with his words, and bountifully with his whip, never using the former where the latter would answer as well**. When he whipped, he seemed to do so from a sense of duty, and feared no consequences. He did nothing reluctantly, no matter how disagreeable; always at his post, never inconsistent. He always promised to fulfill. He was, in a word, a man of the most inflexible firmness and stone-like coolness.

His savage barbarity was equalled only by the **consummate** coolness with which he committed the grossest and most savage deeds upon the slaves under his charge. Mr. Gore once undertook to whip one of Colonel Lloyd's slaves, by the name of Demby. He had given Demby a few stripes, when, to get rid of the scourging, he ran and plunged himself into a creek, and stood there at the depth of his shoulders, refusing to come out. Mr. Gore told him that he would give him three calls, and that, if he did not come out at the third call, he would shoot him. The first call was given. Demby made no response, but stood his ground. The second and third calls were given with the same result.

....

dealt sparingly with his words, and bountifully with his whip, never using the former where the latter would answer as well said very little and chose to beat slaves instead of yelling at them

consummate complete

Mr. Gore then, without consultation or deliberation with anyone, not even giving Demby an additional call, raised his **musket** to his face, taking deadly aim at his standing victim, and in an instant poor Demby was no more. His mangled body sank out of sight, and blood and brains marked the water where he had stood.

A thrill of horror flashed through every soul upon the plantation, excepting Mr. Gore. He alone seemed **cool and collected**. He was asked by Colonel Lloyd and my old master, why he resorted to this extraordinary expedient. His reply was (as well as I can remember), that Demby had become unmanageable. He was setting a dangerous example to the other slaves—one which, if **suffered to pass without some such** demonstration on his part, would finally lead to the **total subversion** of all rule and order upon the plantation. He argued that if one slave refused to be corrected and escaped with his life, the other slaves would soon copy the example; the result of which would be the freedom of the slaves and the enslavement of the whites. Mr. Gore's defense was satisfactory. He was continued in his station as overseer upon the home plantation.

....

musket gun
cool and collected calm and relaxed
suffered to pass without some such he did not show a
total subversion end

CHAPTER V

As to my own treatment while I lived on Colonel Lloyd's plantation, it was very similar to that of the other slave children. I was not old enough to work in the field, and there being little else than field work to do, I had a great deal of **leisure** time. The most I had to do was to drive up the cows at evening, keep the **fowls** out of the garden, keep the front yard clean, and run errands for my old master's daughter, Mrs. Lucretia Auld. Most of my leisure time I spent helping Master Daniel Lloyd in finding his birds, after he had shot them. My connection with Master Daniel was of some advantage to me. He **became quite attached to** me, and was a sort of protector of me. He would not allow the older boys to **impose upon** me, and would divide his cakes with me.

I was seldom whipped by my old master, and suffered little from anything else than hunger and cold. I suffered much from hunger, but much more from cold.

....

leisure free
fowls birds
became quite attached to liked
impose upon bother

In hottest summer and coldest winter, I was kept almost naked—no shoes, no stockings, no jacket, no trousers, nothing on but a coarse tow linen shirt, reaching only to my knees. I had no bed. I **must have perished with** cold, but on the coldest nights, I used to steal a bag which was used for carrying corn to the mill. I would crawl into this bag, and sleep on the cold, damp, clay floor, with my head in and feet out. My feet have been so cracked with the frost, that the pen with which I am writing might be laid in the **gashes**.

We were not **regularly allowanced**. Our food was coarse cornmeal boiled. This was called *mush*. It was put into a large wooden tray or trough, and set down upon the ground. The children were then called, like so many pigs, and like so many pigs they would come and devour the mush; some with oystershells, others with pieces of shingle, some with naked hands, and none with spoons. The child that ate fastest got most; the child that was strongest secured the best place; and few left the trough satisfied.

I was probably between seven and eight years old when I left Colonel Lloyd's plantation. I left it with joy.

....

must have perished with would have died from the
gashes deep cuts in my feet
regularly allowanced given food on a regular basis

I shall never forget the **ecstasy** with which I received the **intelligence** that my old master (Anthony) had determined to let me go to Baltimore, to live with Mr. Hugh Auld, brother to my old master's son-in-law, Captain Thomas Auld. I received this information about three days before my departure. They were three of the happiest days I ever enjoyed. I spent the most part of all these three days in the creek, washing off the plantation **scurf**, and preparing myself for my departure.

It was not because I was proud of my appearance. I spent the time in washing, not so much because I wished to, but because Mrs. Lucretia had told me I must get all the dead skin off my feet and knees before I could go to Baltimore; for the people in Baltimore were very clean, and would laugh at me if I looked dirty. Besides, she was going to give me a pair of trousers, which I should not put on unless I got all the dirt off me. The thought of owning a pair of trousers was great indeed! It was almost **a sufficient motive**, not only to make me take off what would be called by pig-drovers the **mange**, but the skin itself. I went at it in good earnest, working for the first time with the

....

ecstasy complete happiness
intelligence information
scurf dirt
a sufficient motive enough of a reason
mange diseased skin

hope of reward.

The ties that ordinarily bind children to their homes were **all suspended** in my case. I **found no severe trial in** my departure. My home was charmless; it was not home to me; on parting from it, I could not feel that I was leaving anything which I could have enjoyed by staying. My mother was dead, my grandmother lived far off, so I seldom saw her. I had two sisters and one brother, that lived in the same house with me; but the early separation of us from our mother had **well-nigh blotted** the fact of our relationship from our memories. I looked for home elsewhere, and was sure nothing could be worse than the one which I was leaving. If, however, I found in my new home hardship, hunger, whipping, and nakedness, I had the consolation that I should not have escaped any one of them by staying. Having already had more than a taste of them in the house of my old master, and having endured them there, I very naturally **inferred my ability to** endure them elsewhere, and especially at Baltimore; for I had a feeling about Baltimore that is expressed in the proverb, that "being hanged in England is preferable to dying

....

all suspended not there
found no severe trial in was happy about
well-nigh blotted almost erased
inferred my ability to believed I could

a natural death in Ireland." I had the strongest desire to see Baltimore. Cousin Tom, though not fluent in speech, had inspired me with that desire by his eloquent description of the place. I could never point out anything at the Great House, no matter how beautiful or powerful, that could compare to what he had seen in Baltimore, both in beauty and strength. Even the Great House itself, with all its pictures, was far inferior to many buildings in Baltimore. **So strong was my desire, that I thought a gratification of it would fully compensate for whatever loss of comforts I should sustain by the exchange.** I left without a regret, and with the highest hopes of future happiness.

We sailed out of Miles River for Baltimore on a Saturday morning. I remember only the day of the week, for at that time I had no knowledge of the days of the month, nor the months of the year. On setting sail, I walked aft, and gave to Colonel Lloyd's plantation what I hoped would be the last look. I then placed myself in the bows of the sloop, and there spent the remainder of the day in looking ahead, interesting myself in what was in the distance rather than in things near by or behind.

....

So strong was my desire, that I thought a gratification of it would fully compensate for whatever loss of comforts I should sustain by the exchange. I was so eager to leave, that I was willing to risk losing the comforts I had.

In the afternoon of that day, we reached Annapolis, the capital of the State. We stopped but a few moments, so that I had no time to go on shore. It was the first large town that I had ever seen, and though it would look small compared with some of our New England factory villages, I thought it a wonderful place for its size—more imposing even than the Great House Farm!

We arrived at Baltimore early on Sunday morning, landing at Smith's Wharf, not far from Bowley's Wharf. We had on board the sloop a large flock of sheep; and after aiding in driving them to the slaughterhouse of Mr. Curtis on Louden Slater's Hill, I was **conducted** by Rich, one of the **hands** belonging on board of the sloop, to my new home in Alliciana Street, near Mr. Gardner's shipyard, on Fells Point.

Mr. and Mrs. Auld were both at home, and met me at the door with their little son Thomas, **to take care of whom I had been given**. And here I saw what I had never seen before; it was a white face beaming with the most kindly emotions; it was the face of my new mistress, Sophia Auld. I wish I could describe the rapture that flashed through my soul as I beheld it. It

....

conducted guided

hands slaves

to take care of whom I had been given who I would care for was a new and strange sight to me, brightening up my pathway with the light of happiness. Little Thomas was told, there was his Freddy—and I was told to take care of little Thomas; and thus I entered upon the duties of my new home with the most cheering prospect ahead.

I look upon my departure from Colonel Lloyd's plantation as one of the most interesting events of my life. It is possible, and even quite probable, that **but for the mere circumstance** of being removed from that plantation to Baltimore, I should have today, instead of being here seated by my own table, in the enjoyment of freedom and the happiness of home, writing this Narrative, been **confined in the galling** chains of slavery. Going to live at Baltimore laid the foundation, and opened the gateway, to all my **subsequent prosperity**. I have ever regarded it as the first plain **manifestation of that kind providence** which I have ever had. It marked my life with so many favors. I regarded the selection of myself as being somewhat remarkable. There were a number of slave children that

....

but for the mere circumstance if not for the chance
confined in the galling left in the horrible
subsequent prosperity later achievements
manifestation of that kind of providence bit of luck

might have been sent from the plantation to Baltimore. There were those younger, those older, and those of the same age. I was chosen from among them all, and was the first, last, and only choice.

BEFORE YOU MOVE ON...

1. **Cause and Effect** Why did slaves lie about their masters being kind?

2. **Inference** The proverb on pages 43–44 means it is better to be killed in a place you love than to die naturally in a place you hate. What does this show about how Frederick felt about his life?

LOOK AHEAD Read Chapters 6–7 to see how Frederick found the key to freedom.

CHAPTER VI

My new mistress proved to be all she appeared when I first met her at the door—a woman of the kindest heart and finest feelings. She had never had a slave under her control previously to myself, and prior to her marriage she had been dependent upon her **own industry for a living**. She was by trade a weaver; and because she stayed busy, she had been **in a good degree preserved from** the blighting and dehumanizing effects of slavery. I was utterly astonished at her goodness. I scarcely knew how to behave towards her. She was entirely unlike any other white woman I had ever seen. I could not approach her as I was accustomed to approach other white ladies. My early instruction was all out of place. The **crouching servility**, usually so acceptable a quality in a slave, did not please her. Her favor was not gained by it; she seemed to be disturbed by it. She did not deem it **impudent or unmannerly** for a slave to look her in

....

own industry for a living own work to make money
in a good degree preserved from untouched by
crouching servility extreme polite behavior
impudent or unmannerly rude

the face. The meanest slave was put fully at ease in her presence, and none left without feeling better for having seen her. Her face was made of heavenly smiles, and her voice of tranquil music.

But, alas! this kind heart had but a short time to remain such. **The fatal poison of irresponsible power was already in her hands, and soon commenced its infernal work.** That cheerful eye, under the influence of slavery, soon became red with rage; that voice, made all of sweet accord, changed to one of harsh and horrid discord; and that angelic face gave place to that of a demon.

Very soon after I went to live with Mr. and Mrs. Auld, she very kindly commenced to teach me the A, B, C. After I had learned this, she assisted me in learning to spell words of three or four letters. Just at this point of my progress, Mr. Auld found out what was going on, and at once forbade Mrs. Auld to instruct me further, telling her, among other things, that it was unlawful, as well as unsafe, to teach a slave to read. To use his own words, further, he said, "If you give a nigger **an inch, he will take an ell**. A nigger should

---

The fatal poison of irresponsible power was already in her hands, and soon commenced its infernal work. The power of slavery made the mistress change from being nice to angry and mean.

an inch, he will take an ell a little, he'll want more

know nothing but to obey his master—to do as he is told to do. Learning would *spoil* the best nigger in the world. Now," said he, "if you teach that nigger (speaking of myself) how to read, there would be no keeping him. It would forever unfit him to be a slave. He would at once become unmanageable, and of no value to his master. As to himself, it could do him no good, but a great deal of harm. It would make him discontented and unhappy." These words sank deep into my heart, stirred up **sentiments within that lay slumbering**, and called into existence an entirely new train of thought. It was a new and special **revelation**, explaining dark and mysterious things, that in my youth, I had struggled to understand, but struggled in vain. I now understood what had been to me **a most perplexing difficulty—to wit**, the white man's power to enslave the black man. It was a grand achievement, and I prized it highly. From that moment, I understood the pathway from slavery to freedom. It was just what I wanted, and I got it at a time when I least expected it. Whilst I was saddened by the thought of losing the aid of my kind mistress, I was gladdened by

....

sentiments within that lay slumbering feelings that had been quiet inside me

revelation discovery

a most perplexing difficulty—to wit a very difficult idea to understand—that is the invaluable instruction which, by the merest accident, I had gained from my master. Though **conscious of** the difficulty of learning without a teacher, I set out with high hope, and a fixed purpose, at whatever cost of trouble, to learn how to read. The very decided manner with which he spoke, and strove to impress his wife with the evil consequences of giving me instruction, served to convince me that he was deeply sensible of the truths he was uttering. It gave me the best assurance that I might rely with the utmost confidence on the results which, he said, would flow from teaching me to read. What he most **dreaded**, I most desired. What he most loved, I most hated. That which to him was a great evil, to be carefully **shunned**, was to me a great good, to be diligently sought; and the argument which he so warmly urged, against my learning to read, only served to inspire me with a desire and determination to learn. In learning to read, I owe almost as much to the bitter opposition of my master, as to the kindly aid of my mistress. I acknowledge the benefit of both.

I had **resided** but a short time in Baltimore before I observed a marked difference in the treatment of

....

conscious of knowing
dreaded feared
shunned avoided
resided lived

slaves from that which I had witnessed in the country. A city slave is almost a freeman compared with a slave on the plantation. He is much better fed and clothed, and enjoys privileges altogether unknown to the slave on the plantation. There is a **vestige of decency**, a sense of shame, that does much to curb and check those outbreaks of **atrocious** cruelty so commonly enacted upon the plantation. He is a desperate slaveholder, who will shock the humanity of his non-slaveholding neighbors with the cries of his lacerated slave. Few are willing to **incur the odium attaching to the reputation of being a cruel master**; and above all things, they would not be known as not giving a slave enough to eat. Every city slave-holder is anxious to have it known of him that he feeds his slaves well; and it is due to them to say, that most of them do give their slaves enough to eat. There are, however, some painful exceptions to this rule. Directly opposite to us, on Philpot Street, lived Mr. Thomas Hamilton. He owned two slaves. Their names were Henrietta and Mary. Henrietta was about twenty-two years of age, Mary was about fourteen; and of all the mangled and

....

vestige of decency rule of good treatment

atrocious the worst

incur the odium attaching to the reputation of being a cruel master be hated because they are cruel masters

emaciated creatures I ever saw, these two were the most so. His heart must be harder than stone, that could look at these women and not be moved. The head, neck, and shoulders of Mary were literally cut to pieces. I have frequently felt her head, and found it nearly covered with **festering sores**, caused by the lash of her cruel mistress. I do not know that her master ever whipped her, but I have been an eye-witness to the cruelty of Mrs. Hamilton. I used to be in Mr. Hamilton's house nearly every day. Mrs. Hamilton used to sit in a large chair in the middle of the room, with a heavy cowskin always by her side, and **scarce an hour passed during the day but** was marked by the blood of one of these slaves. The girls seldom passed her without her saying, "Move faster, you *black gip*!" at the same time giving them a blow with the cowskin over the head or shoulders, often drawing the blood. She would then say, "Take that, you *black gip*!"—continuing, "If you don't move faster, I'll move you!" Added to the cruel lashings to which these slaves were subjected, they were kept nearly half-starved. They seldom knew what it was to eat a full meal. I have seen Mary **contending**

....

emaciated creatures starving people
festering sores open wounds
scarce an hour passed during the day but often her whip
contending fighting

with the pigs for the **offal** thrown into the street. So much was Mary kicked and cut to pieces, that she was oftener called *"pecked"* than by her name.

---

offal intestines
"pecked" "chewed"

CHAPTER VII

I lived in Master Hugh's family about seven years. During this time, I succeeded in learning to read and write. To accomplish this, I was compelled to resort to various stratagems. I had no regular teacher. My mistress, who had kindly commenced to instruct me, had, in **compliance with** the advice and direction of her husband, not only ceased to instruct, but had **set her face against my being** instructed by anyone else. Nothing seemed to make her more angry than to see me with a newspaper. She seemed to think that was dangerous. I have had her rush at me with a face made all up of fury, and snatch from me a newspaper, in a manner that **fully revealed her apprehension**. She was an apt woman; and a little experience soon demonstrated, to her satisfaction, that education and

....

compliance with listening to
set her face against my being decided not to let me be
fully revealed her apprehension showed her fear

slavery **were incompatible** with each other.

From this time I was most narrowly watched. If I was in a separate room any considerable length of time, I was sure to be suspected of having a book, and was at once called to give an account of myself. All this, however, was too late. The first step had been taken. Mistress, in teaching me the alphabet, had given me the *inch*, and no precaution could prevent me from taking the *ell*.

The plan which I adopted, and the one by which I was most successful, was that of making friends with all the little white boys whom I met in the street. I **converted** as many of these boys as I could into teachers. With their kindly aid, obtained at different times and in different places, I finally succeeded in learning to read. When I was sent on errands, I always took my book with me, and by doing one part of my errand quickly, I found time to get a lesson before my return. I used also to carry bread with me, enough of which was always in the house, and to which I was always welcome; for I was much better off in this regard than many of the poor white children in our

....

were incompatible did not belong
converted made

neighborhood. This bread I used to **bestow upon** the hungry **little urchins**, who, in return, would give me that more valuable **bread of knowledge**. I am strongly tempted to give the names of two or three of those little boys, as a testimonial of the gratitude and affection I feel toward them; but prudence forbids;—not that it would injure me, but it might embarrass them; for it is almost an **unpardonable offense** to teach slaves to read in this Christian country. It is enough to say of the dear little fellows, that they lived on Philpot Street, very near Durgin and Bailey's ship-yard. I used to talk about slavery with them. I would sometimes say to them, I wished I could be as free as they would be when they got to be men. "You will be free as soon as you are twenty-one, *but I am a slave for life!* Have not I as good a right to be free as you have?" These words used to trouble them; they would express for me the liveliest sympathy, and console me with the hope that something would occur by which I might be free.

I was now about twelve years old, and the thought of being *a slave for life* began to bear heavily upon my heart. Just about this time, I got hold of a book entitled

....

bestow upon give to
little urchins street children
bread of knowledge lesson of learning
unpardonable offense unforgivable crime

"The Columbian Orator." Every opportunity I got, I used to read this book. Among much of other interesting matter, I found in it a dialogue between a master and his slave. The slave was represented as having run away from his master three times. The dialogue represented the conversation which took place between them when the slave was retaken the third time. In this dialogue, the whole argument in behalf of slavery was brought forward by the master, all of which was **disposed of** by the slave. The slave was made to say some very smart as well as impressive things in reply to his master—things which had the desired though unexpected effect; for the conversation resulted in the **voluntary emancipation** of the slave on the part of the master.

In the same book, I met with one of Sheridan's mighty speeches about and in favor of Catholic emancipation. These were choice documents to me. I read them over and over again with unabated interest. They **gave tongue to** interesting thoughts of my own soul, which had frequently flashed through my mind, and died away for want of utterance. The moral which I gained from the dialogue was the power of truth over

....

disposed of argued against
voluntary emancipation freedom without force
gave tongue to made me speak aloud

the conscience of even a slaveholder. What I got from Sheridan was a bold **denunciation** of slavery, and a powerful **vindication** of human rights. The reading of these documents enabled me to utter my thoughts, and to meet the arguments brought forward to sustain slavery; but while they relieved me of one difficulty, they brought on another even more painful than the one of which I was relieved. The more I read, the more I was led to **abhor and detest** my enslavers. I could regard them in no other light than a band of successful robbers, who had left their homes, and gone to Africa, and stolen us from our homes, and in a strange land reduced us to slavery. I **loathed** them as being the meanest as well as the most wicked of men.

I often found myself regretting my own existence, and wishing myself dead. If it wasn't for the hope of being free, I have no doubt but that I should have killed myself, or done something for which I should have been killed. While in this state of mind, I was eager to hear anyone speak of slavery. I was a ready listener. Every little while, I could hear something about the abolitionists. It was some time before I found

....

denunciation rejection
vindication acceptance
abhor and detest passionately hate
loathed hated

what the word meant. It was always used in a way that made it an interesting word to me. If a slave ran away and succeeded in getting clear, or if a slave killed his master, set fire to a barn, or did anything very wrong in the mind of a slaveholder, it was spoken of as the **fruit** of *abolition*. Hearing the word in this connection very often, I set about learning what it meant. The dictionary afforded me little or no help. I found it was "the act of abolishing;" but then I did not know what was to be abolished. Here I was perplexed. I did not dare to ask anyone about its meaning, for I was satisfied that it was something they wanted me to know very little about. After a patient waiting, I got one of our city papers, containing an account of the number of petitions from the North, praying for the abolition of slavery in the District of Columbia, and of the slave trade between the States. From this time I understood the words *abolition* and *abolitionist*, and always listened carefully when that word was spoken, expecting to hear something of importance to myself and fellow-slaves. **The light broke in upon me by degrees.** I went one day down on the wharf of Mr. Waters; and

....

fruit result

The light broke in upon me by degrees. I slowly understood the importance of abolition.

seeing two Irishmen unloading a **scow** of stone, I went, unasked, and helped them. When we had finished, one of them came to me and asked me if I were a slave. I told him I was. He asked, "Are ye a slave for life?" I told him that I was. The good Irishman seemed to be deeply affected by the statement. He said to the other that it was a pity so fine a little fellow as myself should be a slave for life. He said it was a shame to hold me. They both advised me to run away to the North; that I should find friends there, and that I should be free. I pretended not to be interested in what they said, and treated them as if I did not understand them; for I feared they might be **treacherous**. White men have been known to encourage slaves to escape, and then, to get the reward, catch them and return them to their masters. I was afraid that these seemingly good men might use me so; but I nevertheless remembered their advice, and from that time I **resolved** to run away. I looked forward to a time at which it would be safe for me to escape. I was too young to think of doing so immediately; besides, I wished to learn how to write, as I might have **occasion** to write my own **pass**. I consoled myself with the hope

....

scow shipment
treacherous dangerous and not to be trusted
resolved decided
occasion the opportunity
pass document

that I should one day find a good chance. Meanwhile, I would learn to write.

The idea as to how I might learn to write was suggested to me by being in Durgin and Bailey's shipyard, and frequently seeing the ship carpenters, after **hewing**, and getting a piece of timber ready for use, write on the timber the name of that part of the ship for which it was intended. When a piece of timber was intended for the **larboard** side, it would be marked thus—"L." When a piece was for the **starboard** side, it would be marked thus—"S." A piece for the larboard side forward, would be marked thus—"L. F." When a piece was for starboard side forward, it would be marked thus—"S. F." For larboard aft, it would be marked thus—"L. A." For starboard aft, it would be marked thus—"S. A." I soon learned the names of these letters, and for what they were intended when placed upon a piece of timber in the shipyard. I immediately commenced copying them, and in a short time was able to make the four letters named. After that, when I met with any boy who I knew could write, I would tell him I could write as well as he. The next word would

<hr />

hewing cutting wood
larboard left
starboard right

be, "I don't believe you. Let me see you try it." I would then make the letters which I had been so fortunate as to learn, and ask him to **beat that**. In this way I got a good many lessons in writing, which it is quite possible I should never have gotten in any other way. During this time, my **copybook** was the board fence, brick wall, and pavement; my pen and ink was a lump of chalk. With these, I learned mainly how to write. I then commenced and continued copying the Italics in Webster's Spelling Book, until I could make them all without looking in the book. By this time, my little Master Thomas had gone to school, and learned how to write, and had written over a number of copybooks. These had been brought home, and shown to some of our near neighbors, and then laid aside. My mistress used to go to class meeting at the Wilk Street meetinghouse every Monday afternoon, and leave me to take care of the house. When **left thus**, I used to spend the time in writing in the spaces left in Master Thomas's copybook,

....

beat that write better than I did
copybook notebook
left thus she left like this

copying what he had written. I continued to do this until I could write **a hand very similar to that of** Master Thomas. Thus, after **a long, tedious effort** for years, I finally succeeded in learning how to write.

....

a hand very similar to that of letters and words just like
a long, tedious effort trying hard

BEFORE YOU MOVE ON...

1. **Theme** On page 51, what caused Frederick to want to be literate? How is this related to the theme of Education?

2. **Paraphrase** Reread page 49 and 56. What did Frederick mean when he said nothing could stop him "from taking the *ell*"?

LOOK AHEAD Read Chapters 8–9 to see how slavery made people into "animals."

CHAPTER VIII

In a very short time after I went to live at Baltimore, my old master's youngest son Richard died; and in about three years and six months after his death, my old master, Captain Anthony, died, leaving only his son, Andrew, and daughter, Lucretia, to share his estate. I was immediately sent for, to **be valued** with the other property. Here again my feelings rose up in detestation of slavery. I had now a new **conception of my degraded condition**. Prior to this, I had become, if not insensible to my lot, at least partly so. I left Baltimore with a young heart **overborne** with sadness, and a soul full of apprehension. I took passage with Captain Rowe, in the schooner Wild Cat, and, after a sail of about twenty-four hours, I found myself near the place of my birth. I had now been absent from it almost, if not quite, five years. I, however, remembered the place very well. I was only about five years old when I left it to go and live with my old master on Colonel

....

be valued find out my worth

conception of my degraded condition understanding of my low, less-than-human state

overborne filled, overwhelmed

Lloyd's plantation; so that I was now between ten and eleven years old.

We were all ranked together at the **valuation**. Men and women, old and young, married and single, were ranked with horses, sheep, and swine. There were horses and men, cattle and women, pigs and children, all holding the same rank in the scale of being, and we were all **subjected to** the same narrow examination. Silvery-headed age and sprightly youth, maids and matrons, had to undergo the same **indelicate inspection**. At this moment, I saw more clearly than ever the brutalizing effects of slavery upon both slave and slaveholder.

After the valuation, then came the division. I have no language to express the high excitement and deep anxiety which were felt among us poor slaves during this time. Our fate for life was now to be decided. We had no more voice in that decision than the **brutes** among whom we were ranked. A single word from the white men was enough—against all our wishes, prayers, and entreaties—to end forever the dearest friendships, dearest kindred, and strongest ties known

----

valuation sale
subjected to part of
indelicate inspection unpleasant examination
brutes animals

to human beings. In addition to the pain of separation, there was the horrid dread of falling into the hands of Master Andrew. He was known to us all as being a most cruel wretch—a common drunkard, who had, by his **reckless mismanagement and profligate dissipation**, already wasted a large portion of his father's property. We all felt that we might as well be sold at once to the Georgia traders, as to pass into his hands; for we knew that that would be our inevitable condition—a condition held by us all in the utmost horror and dread.

I suffered more anxiety than most of my fellow-slaves. I had known what it was to be kindly treated; they had known nothing of the kind. They had seen little or nothing of the world. They were in very deed men and women of sorrow, and acquainted with grief. Their backs had been **made familiar with the bloody lash, so that they had become callous**; mine was yet tender; for while at Baltimore I got few whippings, and few slaves could boast of a kinder master and mistress than myself; and the thought of passing out of their hands into those of Master Andrew—a

....

reckless mismanagement and profligate dissipation poor organization and wild spending

made familiar with the bloody lash, so that they had become callous whipped so often that their skin was hard

man who, but a few days before, to give me a sample of his bloody disposition, took my little brother by the throat, threw him on the ground, and with the heel of his boot stamped upon his head till the blood **gushed** from his nose and ears—was **well-calculated** to make me anxious as to my fate. After he had committed this savage outrage upon my brother, he turned to me, and said that was the way he meant to serve me one of these days—meaning, I suppose, when I came into his possession.

Thanks to a kind providence, I fell to the **portion** of Mrs. Lucretia, and was sent immediately back to Baltimore, to live again in the family of Master Hugh. Their joy at my return equalled their sorrow at my departure. It was a glad day to me. I had escaped a fate worse than lion's jaws. I was absent from Baltimore, for the purpose of valuation and division, just about one month, and it seemed to have been six.

Very soon after my return to Baltimore, my mistress, Lucretia, died, leaving her husband and one child, Amanda; and in a very short time after her death, Master Andrew died. Now all the property of my old master,

----

gushed came out heavily; poured
well-calculated trying
portion care

slaves included, was in the hands of strangers—strangers who had had nothing to do with **accumulating it**. Not a slave was left free. All remained slaves, from the youngest to the oldest, including my poor old grandmother. She had served my old master faithfully from youth to old age. She had rocked him in infancy, attended him in childhood, served him through life, and at his death **wiped from his icy brow the cold death-sweat, and closed his eyes forever**. She was nevertheless left a slave—a slave for life—a slave in the hands of strangers; and in their hands she saw her children, her grandchildren, and her great-grandchildren, divided, like so many sheep.

In about two years after the death of Mrs. Lucretia, Master Thomas married his second wife. Her name was Rowena Hamilton. She was the eldest daughter of Mr. William Hamilton. Master now lived in St. Michael's. Not long after his marriage, a misunderstanding took place between himself and Master Hugh; and as a means of punishing his brother, he took me from him to live with himself at St. Michael's. Here I underwent another most painful

---

accumulating it my master's family

wiped from his icy brow the cold death-sweat, and closed his eyes forever cared for him until he died

separation. It, however, was not so severe as the one I dreaded at the division of property; for, during this interval, a great change had taken place in Master Hugh and his once kind and affectionate wife. The influence of **brandy upon** him, and of slavery upon her, had effected a disastrous change in the characters of both; so that, as far as they were concerned, I thought I had little to lose by the change. But it was not to them that I was attached. It was to those little Baltimore boys that I felt the strongest attachment. I had received many good lessons from them, and was still receiving them, and the thought of leaving them was painful indeed. I was leaving, too, without the hope of ever being allowed to return. Master Thomas had said he would never let me return again. The **barrier betwixt** himself and brother he considered **impassable**.

I then had to regret that I did not at least make the attempt to carry out my resolution to run away; for the chances of success are **tenfold** greater from the city than from the country.

I sailed from Baltimore for St. Michael's in the sloop Amanda, Captain Edward Dodson. On my passage,

....

brandy upon too much alcohol on
barrier betwixt problems between
impassable unable to fix
tenfold ten times

I paid particular attention to the direction which the steamboats took to go to Philadelphia. I found, instead of going down, when they reached North Point they went up the bay, in a northeasterly direction. I deemed this knowledge **of the utmost importance**. My determination to run away was again **revived**. I resolved to wait only **so long as the offering of a favorable opportunity**. When that came, I was determined to be off.

....

of the utmost importance very useful

revived strong, renewed

so long as the offering of a favorable opportunity until a good chance came

CHAPTER IX

I have now reached a period of my life when I can give dates. I left Baltimore and went to live with Master Thomas Auld at St. Michael's in March 1832. He was to me a new master, and I to him a new slave. I was ignorant of his **temper and disposition**; he was equally so of mine. A very short time, however, brought us into full acquaintance with each other. I was made acquainted with his wife not less than with himself. They were well matched, being equally mean and cruel. I was now, for the first time during a space of more than seven years, made to feel the painful **gnawings** of hunger. I have said Master Thomas was a mean man. He really was. Not to give a slave enough to eat is regarded as the most **aggravated development of** meanness even among slaveholders. The rule is, no matter how coarse the food, only let there be enough of it. This is the theory; and in the part of Maryland from which I came, it is **the general practice**—though

....

temper and disposition personality; way of acting

gnawings feelings

aggravated development of terrible kind of

the general practice common to feed slaves well

there are many exceptions. Master Thomas gave us enough of neither coarse nor fine food. There were four slaves in the kitchen—my sister Eliza, my aunt Priscilla, Henny, and myself; and we were allowed less than a half of a bushel of cornmeal per week, and very little else, either in the shape of meat or vegetables. It was not enough for us to **subsist upon**. We were therefore reduced to the wretched necessity of living at the expense of our neighbors. This we did by begging and stealing, whichever came handy in the time of need, the one being considered **as legitimate as** the other. A great many times have we poor creatures been **nearly perishing** with hunger, when so much food was rotting in the safe and smokehouse, and our pious mistress was aware of the fact; and yet that mistress and her husband would kneel every morning, and pray that God would bless them in basket and store!

Bad as all slaveholders are, we seldom meet one **destitute of every** element of character commanding respect. My master was one of this rare sort. I do not know of one single noble act ever performed by him. The leading trait in his character was meanness; and if

----

subsist upon live on
as legitimate as equal to
nearly perishing almost dying
destitute of every without a single

there were any other element in his nature, it was made subject to this. He was mean; and, like most other mean men, he lacked the ability to conceal his meanness. He was cruel, but cowardly. He commanded without firmness. In the enforcement of his rules, he was at times rigid, and at times **lax**. At times, he spoke to his slaves with the firmness of **Napoleon** and the fury of a demon; at other times, he might well be mistaken for an inquirer who had lost his way. He did nothing of himself. In August, 1832, my master attended a Methodist campmeeting held in the Bayside, Talbot County, and there experienced religion. I indulged a faint hope that his conversion would lead him to emancipate his slaves, and that, if he did not do this, it would, at any rate, make him more kind and humane. I was disappointed in both these respects. It neither made him to be humane to his slaves, nor to emancipate them. If it had any effect on his character, it made him more cruel and hateful in all his ways; for I believe him to have been a much worse man after his conversion than before. Prior to his conversion, he relied upon his own

....

lax not as strict

Napolean a strong ruler

depravity to shield and sustain him in his savage barbarity; but after his conversion, **he found religious sanction and support for** his slaveholding cruelty.

While I lived with my master in St. Michael's, there was a white young man, a Mr. Wilson, who proposed to keep a Sabbath school for the instruction of such slaves as might be disposed to learn to read the New Testament. We had met only three times, when Mr. West and Mr. Fairbanks, both classleaders, with many others, came upon us with sticks and other missiles, drove us off, and forbade us to meet again. Thus ended our little Sabbath school in the pious town of St. Michael's.

I have said my master found religious sanction for his cruelty. As an example, I will state one of many facts going to prove the charge. I have seen him tie up a **lame** young woman, and whip her with a heavy cowskin upon her naked shoulders, causing the warm red blood to drip; and, in justification of the bloody deed, he would quote this passage of Scripture—"He that knoweth his master's will, and doeth it not, shall be beaten with many stripes."

....

depravity to shield and sustain him in his savage barbarity evil to treat slaves with extreme cruelty

he found religious sanction and support for he used God as an excuse to continue

lame disabled

Master would keep this lacerated young woman tied up in this horrid situation four or five hours at a time. I have known him to tie her up early in the morning, and whip her before breakfast; leave her, go to his store, return at dinner, and whip her again, cutting her in the places already made raw with his cruel lash. The secret of master's cruelty toward "Henny" is found in the fact of her being almost helpless. When quite a child, she fell into the fire, and burned herself horribly. Her hands were so burnt that she never got the use of them. She could do very little but **bear heavy burdens**. She was to master **a bill of expense**; and since he was a mean man, she was a constant offense to him. He seemed desirous of getting the poor girl out of existence. He gave her away once to his sister; but, being a poor gift, she was not disposed to keep her. Finally, my benevolent master, to use his own words, "set her adrift to take care of herself." Here was a recently-converted man, **holding on upon** the mother, and at the same time **turning out** her helpless child, to starve and die! Master Thomas was one of the many pious slaveholders who hold slaves for the very charitable purpose of taking care of them.

....

bear heavy burdens worry often
a bill of expense useless and expensive to keep
holding on upon keeping
turning out letting go of

My master and myself had quite a number of differences. He found me unsuitable to his purpose. My city life, he said, had had a very **pernicious** effect upon me. It had almost ruined me for every good purpose, and fitted me for everything which was bad. One of my greatest faults was that of letting his horse run away, and go down to his father-in-law's farm, which was about five miles from St. Michael's. I would then have to go after it. My reason for this kind of carelessness, or carefulness, was, that I could always get something to eat when I went there. Master William Hamilton, my master's father-in-law, always gave his slaves enough to eat. I never left there hungry, no matter how great the need of my speedy return. Master Thomas at length said he would stand it no longer. I had lived with him nine months, during which time he had given me a number of severe whippings, all to no good purpose. He resolved to put me out, as he said, to be **broken**; and, for this purpose, he **let** me for one year to a man named Edward Covey. Mr. Covey was a poor man, a farm-renter. He rented the place in which he lived, and also rented the workers who **tilled** it. Mr. Covey had

....

pernicious bad
broken well-trained
let gave
tilled farmed

acquired a very high reputation for breaking young slaves, and this reputation was **of immense value** to him. It enabled him to get his farm tilled with much less expense to himself than he could have had it done without such a reputation. Some slaveholders thought it not much loss to allow Mr. Covey to have their slaves one year, for the sake of the training to which they were subjected, without any other **compensation**. He could hire young help with great ease, **in consequence** of this reputation. Added to the natural good qualities of Mr. Covey, he was a professor of religion—a pious soul—a member and a class-leader in the Methodist church. All of this added weight to his reputation as a "nigger-breaker." I was aware of all the facts, having been made acquainted with them by a young man who had lived there. I nevertheless made the change gladly; for I was sure of getting enough to eat, which is **not the smallest consideration** to a hungry man.

---

of immense value very valuable

compensation payment

in consequence because

not the smallest consideration very important

BEFORE YOU MOVE ON...

1. **Paraphrase** On page 66, what did Frederick mean when he said slavery had "brutalizing effects on both slaves and slaveholders"?

2. **Conclusions** Why was Frederick sent to live with a man who had an evil reputation? Why wasn't he scared?

LOOK AHEAD How did Frederick survive his sickness? Read pages 79–102 to find out.

CHAPTER X

I had left Master Thomas's house, and went to live with Mr. Covey, on the 1st of January, 1833. I was now, for the first time in my life, a field hand. In my new employment, I found myself even more awkward than a country boy appeared to be in a large city. I had been at my new home but one week before Mr. Covey gave me a very severe whipping, cutting my back, causing the blood to run, and **raising ridges** on my flesh as large as my little finger. The details of this affair are as follows: Mr. Covey sent me, very early in the morning of one of our coldest days in the month of January, to the woods, to get a load of wood. He gave me a team of **unbroken oxen**. He told me which was the **in-hand ox, and which the off-hand one**. He then tied the end of a large rope around the horns of the in-hand ox, and gave me the other end of it, and told me, if the oxen started to run, that I must hold onto the rope. I had never driven oxen before, and of course I was very

....

raising ridges making cuts and scars

unbroken oxen untrained bulls

in-hand ox, and which the off-hand one bull that turns left and which is the one that turns right

awkward. I, however, succeeded in getting to the edge of the woods with little difficulty; but I had got **a very few rods** into the woods, when the oxen took fright, and **started full tilt**, carrying the cart against trees, and over stumps, in the most frightful manner. I expected every moment that **my brains would be dashed out** against the trees. After running thus for a considerable distance, the oxen finally **upset the cart, dashing** it with great force against a tree, and threw themselves into a dense thicket. How I escaped death, I do not know. There I was, entirely alone, in a thick wood, in a place new to me. My cart was upset and shattered, my oxen were entangled among the young trees, and there was no one to help me. After much effort, I succeeded in getting my cart righted, my oxen disentangled, and again yoked to the cart. I now proceeded with my team to the place where I had, the day before, been chopping wood, and loaded my cart pretty heavily, thinking in this way to tame my oxen. I then proceeded on my way home. I had now consumed one-half of the day. I got out of the woods safely, and now felt out of danger. I stopped my oxen to open the woods gate; and just as

....

a very few rods about thirty feet
started full tilt ran at full speed
my brains would be dashed out I would hit my head
upset the cart, dashing turned over the cart, breaking

I did so, before I could get hold of **my ox-rope**, the oxen again started, rushed through the gate, catching it between the wheel and the body of the cart, tearing it to pieces, and coming within a few inches of crushing me against the gatepost. Thus twice, in one short day, I escaped death by the merest chance. On my return, I told Mr. Covey what had happened, and how it happened. He ordered me to return to the woods again immediately. I did so, and he followed on after me. Just as I got into the woods, he came up and told me to stop my cart, and that he would teach me how to **trifle** away my time, and break gates. He then went to a large gum-tree, and with his axe cut three large **switches**. After trimming them up neatly with his pocketknife, he ordered me to take off my clothes. I did not answer, but stood with my clothes on. He repeated his order. I still did not answer, nor did I move to strip myself. Upon this he **rushed at me** with the fierceness of a tiger, tore off my clothes, and lashed me till he had worn out his switches, cutting me so savagely as to leave the marks visible for a long time after. This whipping was the first of a number just like it, and for similar offenses.

....

my ox-rope the rope used to hold the bulls

trifle waste

switches pieces of thin wood

rushed at me ran towards me

I lived with Mr. Covey one year. During the first six months of that year, barely a week passed without his whipping me. I was seldom free from a sore back. My awkwardness was almost always his excuse for whipping me. We were worked **fully up to the point of endurance**. Long before day we were up, our horses fed, and by the first approach of day we were off to the field with our hoes and ploughing teams. Mr. Covey gave us enough to eat, but barely enough time to eat it. We were often less than five minutes taking our meals. We were often in the field from the first approach of day till its last lingering ray had left us; and at **saving-fodder time, midnight often caught us in the field binding blades**.

Covey would be out with us. The way he used to stand it, was this. He would spend most of his afternoons in bed. He would then come out fresh in the evening, ready to urge us on with his words, example, and frequently with the whip. Mr. Covey was one of the few slaveholders who could and did work with his hands. He was a hardworking man. He knew by himself just what a man or a boy could do. There was no deceiving

....

fully up to the point of endurance until we could not work any more

saving-fodder time, midnight often caught us in the field binding blades midnight, we were still working

him. His work went on in his absence almost as well as in his presence; and he **had the faculty of making us feel that he was ever present with us**. This he did by surprising us. He seldom approached the spot where we were at work openly, if he could do it secretly. He always aimed at taking us by surprise. He was so cunning that we used to call him, among ourselves, "the snake." When we were at work in the cornfield, he would sometimes crawl on his hands and knees to avoid detection, and all at once he would rise nearly in our midst, and scream out, "Ha, ha! Come, come! Dash on, dash on!" This being his mode of attack, it was never safe to stop a single minute. **His comings were like a thief in the night.** He seemed to always be there. He was under every tree, behind every stump, in every bush, and at every window on the plantation. He would sometimes mount his horse, as if bound to St. Michael's, a distance of seven miles, and in half an hour afterwards you would see him **coiled up** in the corner of the wood fence, watching every motion of the slaves. He would, for this purpose, leave his horse tied up in the woods. Again, he would sometimes walk up to us, and give

....

had the faculty of making us feel that he was ever present with us seemed to be everywhere we were

His comings were like a thief in the night. We never knew where he would appear.

coiled up curled up like a snake

us orders as though he was upon the point of starting on a long journey, turn his back upon us, and make as though he was going to the house to get ready; and, before he would get **half way thither**, he would turn short and crawl into a fence corner, or behind some tree, and there watch us till the sun went down.

If at any one time of my life more than another, I was made to **drink the bitterest dregs** of slavery, that time was during the first six months of my stay with Mr. Covey. We were worked in all weathers. It was never too hot or too cold; it could never rain, blow, hail, or snow too hard for us to work in the field. Work, work, work was scarcely more the order of the day than of the night. The longest days were too short for him, and the shortest nights too long for him. I was somewhat unmanageable when I first went there, but a few months of this discipline tamed me. Mr. Covey succeeded in breaking me. I was broken in body, soul, and spirit. **My natural elasticity was crushed, my intellect languished, the disposition to read departed**, the cheerful spark that lingered about my eye died; the dark night of slavery closed in upon me; and behold a man

....

half way thither halfway there

drink the bitterest dregs experience the worst

My natural elasticity was crushed, my intellect languished, the disposition to read departed My hope was gone, and I did not care about learning or reading

transformed into a brute!

Sunday was my only leisure time. I spent this in a sort of beastlike stupor, between sleep and wake, under some large tree. At times I would rise up, a flash of energetic freedom would dart through my soul, accompanied with a faint beam of hope, that flickered for a moment, and then vanished. I sank down again, mourning over my wretched condition. I **was sometimes prompted to take** my life, and that of Covey, but was prevented by a combination of hope and fear. My sufferings on this plantation seem now like a dream rather than a stern reality.

I have already **intimated** that my condition was much worse, during the first six months of my stay at Mr. Covey's, than in the last six. The circumstances leading to the change in Mr. Covey's course toward me **form an epoch in my humble history**. You have seen how a man was made a slave; you shall see how a slave was made a man. On one of the hottest days of the month of August, 1833, Bill Smith, William Hughes, a slave named Eli, and myself, were engaged in fanning wheat. Hughes was clearing the fanned wheat from

....

was sometimes prompted to take thought about ending

intimated said

form an epoch in my humble history began a change in my life

before the fan. Eli was turning, Smith was feeding, and I was carrying wheat to the fan. The work was simple, requiring strength rather than intellect; yet, to one entirely unused to such work, it came very hard. About three o'clock of that day, I **broke down**; my strength failed me; I was seized with a violent aching of the head, attended with extreme dizziness; I trembled in every limb. Finding what was coming, I **nerved myself up**, feeling it would **never do** to stop work. I stood as long as I could **stagger to the hopper** with grain. When I could stand no longer, I fell, and felt as if held down by an immense weight. The fan of course stopped; every one had his own work to do; and no one could do the work of the other, and have his own go on at the same time.

Mr. Covey was at the house, about one hundred yards from the treading-yard where we were fanning. On hearing the fan stop, he left immediately, and came to the spot where we were. He hastily inquired what the matter was. Bill answered that I was sick, and there was no one to bring wheat to the fan. I had by this time crawled away under the side of the post-and-rail fence

....

broke down could no longer work
nerved myself up forced myself to continue working
never do be a bad idea
stagger to the hopper slowly walk to the storage area

that enclosed the yard, hoping to find relief by getting out of the sun. He then asked where I was. He was told by one of the hands. He came to the spot, and, after looking at me awhile, asked me what was the matter. I told him as well as I could, for I **scarce had strength to speak**. He then gave me a savage kick in the side, and told me to get up. I tried to do so, but fell back in the attempt. He gave me another kick, and again told me to rise. I again tried, and succeeded in gaining my feet; but, stooping to get the tub with which I was feeding the fan, I again staggered and fell. While down in this situation, Mr. Covey **took up the hickory slat** with which Hughes had been striking off the half-bushel measure, and with it gave me a heavy blow upon the head, making a large wound, and the blood ran freely. Then again told me to get up. I **made no effort to comply**, having now made up my mind to let him do his worst. In a short time after receiving this blow, my head grew better. Mr. Covey had now left me **to my fate**. At this moment I resolved, for the first time, to go to my master, enter a complaint, and ask his protection. In order to do this, I must that

---

scarce had strength to speak could hardly talk
took up the hickory slat grabbed a wooden board
made no effort to comply did not do what he asked
to my fate alone

afternoon walk seven miles; and this, under the circumstances, was truly a severe undertaking. I was **exceedingly feeble**; made so as much by the kicks and blows which I received, as by the severe fit of sickness to which I had been subjected. I, however, **watched my chance**, while Covey was looking in an opposite direction, and started for St. Michael's. I succeeded in getting a considerable distance on my way to the woods, when Covey discovered me, and called after me to come back, threatening what he would do if I did not come. I disregarded both his calls and his threats, and made my way to the woods as fast as my feeble state would allow; and thinking I might be **overhauled** by him if I **kept** the road, I walked through the woods, keeping far enough from the road to avoid detection, and near enough to prevent losing my way. I had not gone far before my little strength again failed me. I could go no farther. I fell down, and lay for a considerable time. The blood was yet oozing from the wound on my head. For a time I thought I should bleed to death; and think now that I should have done so, but that the blood

....

exceedingly feeble very weak
watched my chance waited to run away
overhauled caught
kept stayed on

so matted my hair as to stop the wound. After lying there about three-quarters of an hour, I nerved myself up again, and started on my way, through bogs and briers, barefooted and bareheaded, tearing my feet sometimes at nearly every step; and after a journey of about seven miles, occupying some five hours to perform it, I arrived at master's store. I looked bad enough to affect anyone unless they had a heart of iron. From the **crown** of my head to my feet, I was covered with blood. My hair was all clotted with dust and blood; my shirt was stiff with blood. I suppose I looked like a man who had escaped a den of wild beasts, and barely escaped them. In this state I appeared before my master, **humbly entreating him to interpose** his authority for my protection. I told him all the circumstances as well as I could, and it seemed, as I spoke, at times to affect him. He would then walk the floor, and seek to justify Covey by saying he expected I deserved it. He asked me what I wanted. I told him, to let me get a new home; that if I lived with Mr. Covey again, I would die with him; that Covey would surely kill me; he was **in a fair way for it**.

....

so matted my hair as to stop made my hair stick to my head and sealed

crown top

humbly entreating him to interpose asking him for

in a fair way for it ready to do it

Master Thomas **ridiculed** the idea that there was any danger of Mr. Covey's killing me, and said that he knew Mr. Covey; that he was a good man, and that he could not think of taking me from him; that, should he do so, he would lose the whole year's wages; that I belonged to Mr. Covey for one year, and that I must go back to him, come what might; and that I must not trouble him with any more stories, or that he would himself *get hold of me.* After threatening me thus, he gave me a very large **dose of salts**, telling me that I might remain in St. Michael's that night, (it being quite late), but that I must be off back to Mr. Covey's early in the morning; and that if I did not, he would *get hold of me*, which meant that he would whip me. I remained all night, and, according to his orders, I started off to Covey's in the morning, (Saturday morning), wearied in body and broken in spirit. I got no supper that night or breakfast that morning. I reached Covey's about nine o'clock; and just as I was getting over the fence that divided Mrs. Kemp's fields from ours, out ran Covey with his cowskin to give me another whipping. Before he could reach me, I succeeded in getting to the cornfield; and as the corn

....

ridiculed laughed at

dose of salts amount of medicine

was very high, it **afforded me the means of hiding**. He seemed very angry, and searched for me a long time. My behavior was altogether **unaccountable**. He finally gave up the chase, thinking, I suppose, that I must come home for something to eat; he would give himself no further trouble in looking for me. I spent that day mostly in the woods, having the alternative before me—to go home and be whipped to death, or stay in the woods and be starved to death. That night, I met Sandy Jenkins, a slave with whom I was somewhat acquainted. Sandy had a free wife who lived about four miles from Mr. Covey's; and it being Saturday, he was on his way to see her. I told him my circumstances, and he very kindly invited me to go home with him. I went home with him, and talked this whole matter over, and got his advice as to what **course it was best for me to pursue**. I found Sandy an old adviser. He told me, with great solemnity, I must go back to Covey; but that before I went, I must go with him into another part of the woods, where there was a certain *root*, which, if I would take some of it with me, carrying it *always on my right side*, would make it impossible for Mr. Covey, or

....

afforded me the means of hiding made it easy for me to hide

unaccountable impossible to explain

course it was best for me to pursue I should do

root plant

any other white man, to whip me. He said he had carried it for years; and since he had done so, he had never received a blow, and never expected to while he carried it. I at first rejected the idea, that the simple carrying of a root in my pocket would have any such effect as he had said, and was not disposed to take it; but Sandy **impressed the necessity with much earnestness**, telling me it could do no harm, if it did no good. To please him, I finally took the root, and, according to his direction, carried it on my right side. This was Sunday morning. I immediately started for home; and upon entering the yard gate, out came Mr. Covey on his way to meeting. He spoke to me very kindly, **bade me** drive the pigs from a lot near by, and passed on towards the church. Now, this singular conduct of Mr. Covey really made me begin to think that there was something in the *root* which Sandy had given me; and had it been on any other day than Sunday, I **could have attributed the conduct to no other cause than** the influence of that root; and as it was, I was half inclined to think the *root* to be something more than I at first had taken it to be. All

....

impressed the necessity with much earnestness said it was very important

bade me told me to

could have attributed the conduct to no other cause than would think that it was only

went well till Monday morning. On this morning, the virtue of the *root* was fully tested. Long before daylight, I was called to go and rub, curry, and feed, the horses. I obeyed, and was glad to obey. But while I was doing this, while I was **throwing down some blades** from the loft, Mr. Covey entered the stable with a long rope; and just as I was half out of the loft, he caught hold of my legs, and wanted to tie me. As soon as I found what he was up to, I jumped, and as I did so, he holding to my legs, I was brought sprawling on the stable floor. Mr. Covey seemed now to think he had me, and could do what he pleased; but at this moment—from **whence came the spirit** I don't know—I resolved to fight; and, **suiting my action to the resolution**, I seized Covey hard by the throat; and as I did so, I rose. He held on to me, and I to him. My resistance was so entirely unexpected that Covey seemed scared. He trembled like a leaf. This gave me assurance, and I held him uneasy, causing the blood to run where I touched him with the ends of my fingers. Mr. Covey soon called out to Hughes for help. Hughes came, and, while Covey held me, attempted to tie my right hand. While he was in

....

throwing down some blades tossing down straw

whence came the spirit where the energy came

suiting my action to the resolution acting on this will to fight

the act of doing so, I watched my chance, and gave him a heavy kick close under the ribs. This kick fairly sickened Hughes, so that he left me in the hands of Mr. Covey. This kick had the effect of not only weakening Hughes, but Covey also. When he saw Hughes bending over with pain, **his courage quailed**. He asked me if I **meant to persist in my resistance**. I told him I did, come what might; that he had used me like a brute for six months, and that I was determined not to be used any longer. With that, he strove to drag me to a stick that was lying just out of the stable door. He meant to knock me down. But just as he was leaning over to get the stick, I seized him with both hands by his collar, and brought him by a sudden **snatch** to the ground. By this time, Bill came. Covey called to him for assistance. Bill wanted to know what he could do. Covey said, "Take hold of him, take hold of him!" Bill said his master hired him out to work, and not to help to whip me; so he left Covey and myself to fight our own battle out. We were at it for nearly two hours. Covey at length let me go, puffing and blowing at a great rate, saying that if I had not resisted, he would not have whipped me at all.

....

his courage quailed Mr. Covey was afraid
meant to persist in my resistance would continue fighting
snatch pull

I considered him as getting entirely the worst end of the bargain; for he had drawn no blood from me, but I had from him. The whole six months afterwards, that I spent with Mr. Covey, he never laid the weight of his finger upon me in anger. He would occasionally say he didn't want to get hold of me again. "No," thought I, "you need not; for you will come off worse than you did before."

This battle with Mr. Covey was the turning-point in my career as a slave. It **rekindled the few expiring embers of freedom**, and revived within me a sense of my own manhood. It recalled the departed self-confidence, and inspired me again with a determination to be free. The gratification afforded by the triumph was a full compensation for whatever else might follow, even death itself. He only can understand the deep satisfaction which I experienced, who has himself **repelled by force the bloody arm of** slavery. I felt as I never felt before. It was a glorious resurrection, from the tomb of slavery, to the heaven of freedom. My long-crushed spirit rose, cowardice departed, **bold defiance took its place**; and I now resolved that, however long I might

....

rekindled the few expiring embers of freedom brought back my desire to be a free man

repelled by force the bloody arm of fought

bold defiance took its place and I wanted to fight back remain a slave in form, the day had passed forever when I could be a slave in fact. I **did not hesitate to let it be known of me**, that the white man who expected to succeed in whipping, must also succeed in killing me.

From this time I was never again what might be called fairly whipped, though I remained a slave four years afterwards. I had several fights, but was never whipped.

It was for a long time a matter of surprise to me why Mr. Covey did not immediately have me taken by the constable to the whipping-post, and there regularly whipped for the crime of raising my hand against a white man in defense of myself. And the only explanation I can now think of does not entirely satisfy me; but such as it is, I will give it. Mr. Covey enjoyed the **most unbounded** reputation for being a first-rate overseer and negro-breaker. It was of considerable importance to him. That reputation was **at stake**; and had he sent me—a boy about sixteen years old—to the public whipping-post, his reputation would have been lost; so, to save his reputation, he **suffered me to** go unpunished.

....

did not hesitate to let it be known of me told everyone

most unbounded strongest

at stake now questionable

suffered me to let me

My term of actual service to Mr. Edward Covey ended on Christmas day, 1833. The days between Christmas and New Year's Day are allowed as holidays; and, accordingly, we were not required to perform any labor, more than to feed and take care of the stock. We considered this time to be our own, by the grace of our masters; and we therefore used or abused it nearly as we pleased. Those of us who had families at a distance, were generally allowed to spend the whole six days **in their society**. This time, however, was spent in various ways. The slaves that were **staid, sober, thinking and industrious** would employ themselves in making corn-brooms, mats, horse-collars, and baskets; and others would spend the time in hunting **opossums, hares, and coons**. But by far most of us engaged in such sports and merriments as playing ball, wrestling, running foot-races, fiddling, dancing, and drinking whisky; and this latter mode of spending the time was by far the most agreeable to the feelings of our masters. A slave who would work during the holidays was considered by our masters as scarcely deserving them. He was regarded as one who rejected the favor of his

....

in their society with them

staid, sober, thinking and industrious serious, clear-headed, thoughtful, and hardworking

opossums, hares, and coons animals

master. It was deemed a disgrace not to get drunk at Christmas; and he was regarded as lazy indeed, who had not provided himself with the necessary means, during the year, to get whisky enough to last him through Christmas.

From what I know of the effect of these holidays upon the slave, I believe them to be among the most effective means in the hands of the slaveholder in keeping down the **spirit of insurrection**. Were the slaveholders at once to abandon this practice, I have not the slightest doubt it would lead to an immediate insurrection among the slaves. These holidays serve as conductors, or safety-valves, to carry off the rebellious spirit of enslaved humanity. **But for these, the slave would be forced up to the wildest desperation**; and woe betide the slaveholder, the day he ventures to remove or hinder the operation of those conductors! I warn him that, in such an event, a spirit will go forth in their midst, more to be dreaded than the most appalling earthquake.

On the first of January, 1834, I left Mr. Covey and went to live with Mr. William Freeland, who

----

spirit of insurrection slave's desire to rebel and overthrow the slaveholders

But for these, the slave would be forced up to the wildest desperation If there were not these times of drinking and relaxing, the slaves would rebel

lived about three miles from St. Michael's. I soon found Mr. Freeland a very different man from Mr. Covey. Though not rich, he was what would be called an educated southern gentleman. Mr. Covey, as I have shown, was a well-trained negro-breaker and slavedriver. The former (slaveholder though he was) seemed to **possess some regard for honor, some reverence for justice**, and some respect for humanity. The latter seemed totally insensible to all such sentiments. Mr. Freeland had many of the faults peculiar to slaveholders, such as being very **passionate and fretful**; but I must do him the justice to say that he was exceedingly free from **those degrading vices** to which Mr. Covey was constantly addicted.

He, like Mr. Covey, gave us enough to eat; but, unlike Mr. Covey, he also gave us sufficient time to take our meals. He worked us hard, but always between sunrise and sunset. He required a good deal of work to be done, but gave us good tools with which to work. His farm was large, but he employed hands enough to work it, and with ease, compared with many of his neighbors. My treatment, while in his employment,

....

possess some regard for honor, some reverence for justice have some good qualities

passionate and fretful emotional and worried

those degrading vices the terrible behavior

was heavenly, compared with what I experienced at the hands of Mr. Edward Covey.

Mr. Freeland was himself the owner of only two slaves. Their names were Henry Harris and John Harris. The **rest of his hands** he hired. These consisted of myself, Sandy Jenkins, and Handy Caldwell. Henry and John were quite intelligent, and in a very little while after I went there, I succeeded in creating in them a strong desire to learn how to read. This desire soon sprang up in the others also. They very soon **mustered up** some old spelling books, and nothing would do but that I must keep a Sabbath school. I agreed to do so, and accordingly devoted my Sundays to teaching these my loved fellow-slaves how to read. Neither of them **knew his letters** when I went there. Some of the slaves of the neighboring farms found what was going on, and also **availed themselves of** this little opportunity to learn to read.

It was understood, among all who came, that there must be as little display about it as possible.

I held my Sabbath school at the house of a free

----

rest of his hands other workers

mustered up found

knew his letters could read or write

availed themselves of used

colored man, whose name I **deem it imprudent** to mention; for should it be known, it might embarrass him greatly, though the crime of holding the school was committed ten years ago. I had at one time over forty scholars, and those of the right sort, ardently desiring to learn. They were of all ages, though mostly men and women. I look back to those Sundays with a great amount of pleasure. They were great days to my soul. The work of instructing my dear fellow-slaves was the sweetest engagement with which I was ever blessed. These dear souls did not come to Sabbath school because it was popular to do so, nor did I teach them because it was good for my reputation. Every moment they spent in that school, they **were liable to be taken up** and given thirty-nine lashes. They came because they wished to learn. Their minds had been **starved** by their cruel masters. They had been **shut up in mental darkness**. I taught them because it was the delight of my soul to be doing something that looked like bettering the condition of my race. I kept up my school nearly the whole year I lived with Mr. Freeland;

....

deem it imprudent think unnecessary
were liable to be taken up risked getting caught
starved unused and kept empty
shut up in mental darkness forced to stay ignorant

and, beside my Sabbath school, I devoted three evenings in the week, during the winter, to teaching the slaves at home. And I have the happiness to know, that several of those who came to Sabbath school learned how to read; and that one, at least, is now free **through my agency**.

....

through my agency because of my teachings

BEFORE YOU MOVE ON...

1. **Sequence** Frederick became sick and could no longer work. What events followed that led to the change in his attitude?

2. **Opinion** Reread pages 97–98. Frederick thought that drinking and relaxing during the holiday held the slaves back. Explain.

LOOK AHEAD Read pages 103–125 to find out if Frederick escaped to freedom.

The year passed off smoothly. It seemed only about half as long as the year which **preceded** it. I went through it without receiving a single blow. I will give Mr. Freeland the credit of being the best master I ever had, *till I became my own master.* **For the ease with which I passed the year, I was, however, somewhat indebted to** the society of my fellow-slaves. They were noble souls; they not only possessed loving hearts, but brave ones. We were linked and interlinked with each other. I loved them with a love stronger than anything I have experienced since. It is sometimes said that we slaves do not love and confide in each other. In answer to this assertion, I can say, I never loved any or confided in any people more than my fellow-slaves, and especially those with whom I lived at Mr. Freeland's. I believe we would have died for each other. We never decided to do anything, of any importance, without **a mutual consultation**. We never moved separately. We were one; and as much so by our tempers and dispositions, as by the mutual hardships to which we were necessarily subjected by our condition as slaves.

....

preceded came before

For the ease with which I passed the year, I was, however, somewhat indebted to The good year was because of

a mutual consultation first talking to each other

At the close of the year 1834, Mr. Freeland again **hired me of my master**, for the year 1835. But, by this time, I began to want to live *upon free land* as well as *with Freeland*; and I was no longer content, therefore, to live with him or any other slaveholder. I began, with the commencement of the year, to prepare myself for a final struggle, which should decide my fate one way or the other. **My tendency was upward.** I was fast approaching manhood, and year after year had passed, and I was still a slave. These thoughts roused me—I must do something. I therefore resolved that 1835 should not pass without witnessing an attempt, on my part, to secure my liberty. But I was not willing to cherish this determination alone. My fellow-slaves were dear to me. I was anxious to have them participate with me in this, my life-giving determination. I therefore, though with great prudence, commenced early to ascertain their views and feelings in regard to their condition, and to **imbue** their minds with thoughts of freedom. I bent myself to devising ways and means for our escape, and meanwhile strove, on all fitting occasions, to impress them with the **gross fraud and inhumanity** of slavery.

....

hired me of my master took me to work for him
My tendency was upward. It was time to run away.
imbue fill
gross fraud and inhumanity lies and unfairness

I went first to Henry, next to John, then to the others. I found, in them all, warm hearts and noble spirits. They were ready to hear, and ready to act when a **feasible plan should be proposed**. This was what I wanted. I talked to them of our want of manhood, if we submitted to our enslavement without at least one noble effort to be free. We met often, and consulted frequently, and told our hopes and fears, recounted the difficulties, real and imagined, which we should be called on to meet. At times we almost gave up, and tried to content ourselves with our wretched lot; at other times, we were firm and unbending in our determination to go. Whenever we suggested any plan, there **was shrinking**—the odds were fearful. Our path was beset with the greatest obstacles; and if we succeeded in gaining the end of it, our right to be free was yet questionable—we were yet liable to be returned to bondage. We could see no spot, this side of the ocean, where we could be free. We knew nothing about Canada. Our knowledge of the North did not extend farther than New York; and to go there, and be forever **harassed with the frightful liability** of being returned to slavery—with the certainty of being

....

feasible plan should be proposed good plan was made
was shrinking were doubts
harassed with the frightful liability afraid

treated tenfold worse than before—the thought was truly a horrible one, and one which it was not easy to overcome.

Sandy, one of our group, **gave up the notion**, but still encouraged us. Our company then consisted of Henry Harris, John Harris, Henry Bailey, Charles Roberts, and myself. Henry Bailey was my uncle, and belonged to my master. Charles married my aunt: he belonged to my master's father-in-law, Mr. William Hamilton.

The plan we finally concluded upon was, to get a large canoe belonging to Mr. Hamilton, and upon the Saturday night previous to Easter holidays, paddle directly up the Chesapeake Bay. On our arrival at the head of the bay, a distance of seventy or eighty miles from where we lived, it was our purpose to **turn our canoe adrift**, and follow the guidance of the North Star till we got beyond the limits of Maryland. Our reason for taking the water route was that we were less liable to be **suspected** as runaways; we hoped to be regarded as fishermen; whereas, if we should take the land route, we should **be subjected to interruptions** of almost every

....

gave up the notion decided not to run away
turn our canoe adrift send our empty boat down the river
suspected thought of
be subjected to interruptions risk creating problems

kind. Any white person who wanted to could stop us and subject us to examination.

The week before our intended start, I wrote several **protections**, one for each of us. As well as I can remember, they were in the following words, to wit:

This is to certify that I, **the undersigned**, have given the bearer, my servant, full liberty to go to Baltimore, and spend the Easter holidays. Written with mine own hand, &c., 1835.

> William Hamilton,
> Near St. Michael's, in Talbot County, Maryland.

We were not going to Baltimore; but, in going up the bay, we went toward Baltimore, and these protections were only intended to protect us while on the bay.

As the time drew near for our departure, our anxiety became more and more intense. **It was truly a matter of life and death with us.** The strength of our determination was about to be fully tested. At this time, I was very active in explaining every difficulty, removing every doubt, dispelling every fear,

....

protections passes, notes

the undersigned William Hamilton

It was truly a matter of life and death with us. We were willing to risk death to be free.

and inspiring all with the firmness indispensable to success in our undertaking; assuring them that **half was gained the instant we made the move**; we had talked long enough; we were now ready to move; if not now, we never should be. And if we did not intend to move now, we might as well fold our arms, sit down, and acknowledge ourselves fit only to be slaves. This, none of us were prepared to acknowledge. Every man stood firm; and at our last meeting, we pledged ourselves afresh, in the most solemn manner, that, at the time appointed, we would certainly start in pursuit of freedom. This was in the middle of the week, at the end of which we were to be off. We went, as usual, to our several fields of labor, but **with bosoms highly agitated with thoughts of our truly hazardous undertaking**. We tried to conceal our feelings as much as possible; and I think we succeeded very well.

After a painful waiting, Saturday morning came, and we were to leave that night. I hailed it with joy, bring what of sadness it might. Friday night was a sleepless one for me. I probably felt more anxious than the rest, because I was, by common consent, at the head

....

half was gained the instant we made the move we were halfway to freedom the moment we ran away

with bosoms highly agitated with thoughts of our truly hazardous undertaking nervous about our escape

of the whole affair. The responsibility of success or failure lay heavily upon me. The glory of the one, and the confusion of the other, would both be mine. The first two hours of that morning were such as I never experienced before, and hope never to again. Early in the morning, we went, as usual, to the field. We were spreading **manure**; and all at once, while thus engaged, I was overwhelmed with an indescribable feeling, in the fullness of which I turned to Sandy, who was near by, and said, "**We are betrayed!**" "Well," said he, "that thought has this moment struck me." We said no more. I was never more certain of anything.

The horn was blown as usual, and we went up from the field to the house for breakfast. I went **for the form**, more than for want of anything to eat that morning. Just as I got to the house, in looking out at the lane gate, I saw four white men, with two colored men. The white men were on horseback, and the colored ones were walking behind, as if tied. I watched them a few moments till they got up to our lane gate. Here they halted, and tied the colored men to the gatepost. I was not yet certain as to what the matter was. In a

....

manure animal waste

We are betrayed! Someone has told the master about our escape plans!

for the form to show things were normal

few moments, in rode Mr. Hamilton, with a speed **betokening** great excitement. He came to the door, and inquired if Master William was in. He was told he was at the barn. Mr. Hamilton, without **dismounting**, rode up to the barn with extraordinary speed. In a few moments, he and Mr. Freeland returned to the house. By this time, the three **constables** rode up, and in great haste dismounted, tied their horses, and met Master William and Mr. Hamilton returning from the barn; and after talking awhile, they all walked up to the kitchen door. There was no one in the kitchen but myself and John. Henry and Sandy were up at the barn. Mr. Freeland put his head in at the door, and called me by name, saying, there were some gentlemen at the door who wished to see me. I stepped to the door, and inquired what they wanted. They at once seized me, and, without giving me any satisfaction, tied me—lashing my hands closely together. I insisted upon knowing what the matter was. They at length said, that they had learned I had been in a "**scrape**," and that I was to be examined before my master; and if their information proved false, I should not be hurt.

....

betokening showing
dismounting getting off his horse
constables policemen
scrape fight

In a few moments, they succeeded in tying John. They then turned to Henry, who had by this time returned, and commanded him to cross his hands. "I won't!" said Henry, in a firm tone, indicating his readiness to meet the consequences of his refusal. "Won't you?" said Tom Graham, the constable. "No, I won't!" said Henry, in a still stronger tone. With this, two of the constables pulled out their shining pistols, and swore, by their Creator, that they would make him cross his hands or kill him. Each **cocked his pistol**, and, with fingers on the trigger, walked up to Henry, saying, at the same time, if he did not cross his hands, they would **blow his damned heart out**. "Shoot me, shoot me!" said Henry; "you can't kill me but once. Shoot, shoot—and be damned! *I won't be tied!*" This he said in a tone of loud defiance; and at the same time, with a motion as quick as lightning, he with one single stroke **dashed the pistols** from the hand of each constable. As he did this, **all hands fell upon him**, and, after beating him some time, they finally overpowered him, and got him tied.

During the scuffle, I managed, I know not how, to

....

cocked his pistol got his gun ready

blow his damned heart out shoot him

dashed the pistols knocked the guns

all hands fell upon him everyone grabbed him

get my pass out, and, without being discovered, put it into the fire. We were all now tied; and just as we were to leave for Easton jail, Betsy Freeland, mother of William Freeland, came to the door with her hands full of biscuits, and divided them between Henry and John. She then delivered a speech, to the following effect—addressing herself to me, she said, "*You devil! You yellow devil!* It was you that put it into the heads of Henry and John to run away. It was all you, you long-legged mulatto devil! Henry nor John would never have thought of such a thing." I made no reply, and was immediately hurried off towards St. Michael's. Just a moment previous to the scuffle with Henry, Mr. Hamilton suggested **the propriety of making a search for the protections** which he had understood Frederick had written for himself and the rest. But, just at the moment he was about **carrying his proposal into effect**, his aid was needed in helping to tie Henry; and the excitement attending the scuffle caused them either to forget, or to deem it unsafe, under the circumstances, to search. So we were not yet **convicted** of the intention to run away.

....

the propriety of making a search for the protections that they first look for the passes

carrying his proposal into effect to search me

convicted found guilty

When we got about half way to St. Michael's, while the constables who had us in charge were looking ahead, Henry inquired of me what he should do with his pass. I told him to eat it with his biscuit, and own nothing; and we passed the word around, "*Own nothing.*" "*Own nothing!*" we all said. Our confidence in each other was unshaken. We were resolved to succeed or fail together, after **the calamity had befallen us as much as before**. We were now prepared for anything. We were to be dragged that morning fifteen miles behind horses, and then to be placed in the Easton jail. When we reached St. Michael's, we underwent a sort of examination. We all denied that we ever intended to run away. We did this more to bring out the evidence against us, than from any hope of getting clear of being sold; for, as I have said, we were ready for that. The fact was, we cared but little where we went, as long as we went together. Our greatest concern was about separation. We dreaded that more than anything this side of death. We found the evidence against us to be the testimony of one person; our master would not tell who it was; but we

....

the calamity had befallen us as much as before our plan had failed

came to a unanimous decision among ourselves as to who their informant was. We were sent off to the jail at Easton. When we got there, we were taken up to the sheriff, Mr. Joseph Graham, and by him placed in jail. Henry, John, and myself, were placed in one room together—Charles and Henry Bailey, in another. Their object in separating us was to **hinder concert**.

We had been in jail scarcely twenty minutes, when a swarm of slave traders and agents for slave traders flocked into jail to look at us, and to ascertain if we were for sale. I never saw such people like this before! I felt myself surrounded by so many **fiends from perdition**. A band of pirates never looked more like their father, the devil. They laughed and grinned over us, saying, "Ah, my boys! We have got you, haven't we?" And after taunting us in various ways, they one by one went into an examination of us, with intent to ascertain our value. They would impudently ask us if we would not like to have them for our masters. We would make them no answer, and leave them to find out as best they could. Then they would curse and swear at us, telling us that they could take the devil out of us in a

....

came to a unanimous decision among ourselves as to who their informant was figured out who had told our master the escape plans

hinder concert stop us from talking to each other

fiends from perdition people from hell

very little while, if we were only in their hands.

While in jail, we found ourselves in much more comfortable quarters than we expected when we went there. We did not get much to eat, nor that which was very good; but we had a good clean room, from the windows of which we could see what was going on in the street, which was very much better than if we had been placed in one of the dark, damp cells. Upon the whole, we got along very well, so far as the jail and its keeper were concerned. Immediately after the holidays were over, **contrary to** all our expectations, Mr. Hamilton and Mr. Freeland came up to Easton, and took Charles, the two Henrys, and John, out of jail, and carried them home, leaving me alone. I regarded this separation as a final one. It caused me more pain than anything else **in the whole transaction**. I was ready for anything rather than separation. I supposed that they had consulted together, and had decided that, **as I was the whole cause of the intention of the others** to run away, it was hard to make the innocent suffer with the guilty; and that they had, therefore, concluded to take the others home, and sell me, as a warning to the

....

contrary to unlike

in the whole transaction that had happened

as I was the whole cause of the intention of the others since I convinced everyone

others that remained. It is due to the noble Henry to say, he seemed almost as **reluctant at** leaving the prison as at leaving home to come to the prison. But we knew we should, in all probability, be separated, if we were sold; and since he was in their hands, he concluded to go **peaceably home**.

I was now left to my fate. I was all alone, and within the walls of a stone prison. But a few days before, and I was full of hope. I expected to have been safe in a land of freedom; but now I was **covered with gloom, sunk down to the utmost despair**. I thought the possibility of freedom was gone. I was kept in the prison about one week, at the end of which, Captain Auld, my master, to my surprise and utter astonishment, came up, and took me out, with the intention of sending me, with a gentleman of his acquaintance, into Alabama. But, for some reason, he did not send me to Alabama, but concluded to send me back to Baltimore, to live again with his brother Hugh, and to learn a trade.

Thus, after an absence of three years and one month, I was once more permitted to return to my old home at Baltimore. My master sent me away, because

....

reluctant at unsure

peaceably home home without a fight

covered with gloom, sunk down to the utmost despair depressed and hopeless

there existed against me a very great prejudice in the community, and he feared I might be killed.

In a few weeks after I went to Baltimore, Master Hugh hired me to Mr. William Gardner, an extensive shipbuilder, on Fell's Point. I was put there to learn how to **calk**. It, however, proved a very unfavorable place to learn to calk. Mr. Gardner was engaged that spring in building two large **man-of-war brigs, professedly** for the Mexican government. The vessels were to be launched in the July of that year, and if this failed, Mr. Gardner was to lose a considerable sum; so that when I entered, all was hurry. There was no time to learn anything. Every man had to do that which he knew how to do. In entering the shipyard, my orders from Mr. Gardner were to do whatever the carpenters commanded me to do. This was placing me at the beck and call of about seventy-five men. I was to regard all these as masters. Their word was to be my law. My situation was a most trying one. At times I needed a dozen pair of hands. I was called a dozen ways in the space of a single minute. Three or four voices would **strike my ear** at the same moment.

....

calk make ships unsinkable
man-of-war brigs, professedly ships, specifically
strike my ear call out to me

It was—"Fred, come help me to **cant** this timber here."—"Fred, come carry this timber yonder."—"Fred, bring that roller here."—"Fred, go get a fresh can of water."—"Fred, come help saw off the end of this timber."—"Fred, go quick, and get the crowbar."—"Fred, hold on the end of this fall."—"Fred, go to the blacksmith's shop, and get a new **punch**."—"Hurra, Fred! run and bring me a cold chisel."—"I say, Fred, bear a hand, and get up a fire as quick as lightning under that steam-box."—"Halloo, nigger! come, turn this grindstone."—"Come, come! move, move! and **bowse this timber** forward."—"I say, darky, blast your eyes, why don't you heat up some pitch?"—"Halloo! halloo! halloo!" (Three voices at the same time.) "Come here!—Go there!—Hold on where you are! Damn you, if you move, I'll knock your brains out!"

This was my school for eight months; and I might have remained there longer, but for a most horrid fight I had with four of the white apprentices, in which my left eye was nearly knocked out, and I was horribly mangled in other respects. The facts in the case were these: Until a very little while after I went there, white and black

....

cant tilt, lean
punch tool
bowse this timber bring this wood
This was my school This is what I learned to do

ship-carpenters worked side by side, and no one seemed to see any **impropriety in it**. All hands seemed to be very well satisfied. Many of the black carpenters were free men. Things seemed to be going on very well. All at once, the white carpenters **knocked off**, and said they would not work with free colored workmen. Their reason for this, as alleged, was, that if free colored carpenters were encouraged, they would soon take the trade into their own hands, and poor white men would be thrown out of employment. They therefore felt called upon at once to put a stop to it. And, taking advantage of Mr. Gardner's necessities, they broke off, swearing they would work no longer, unless he would **discharge** his black carpenters. Now, though this did not extend to me in form, it did reach me in fact. My fellow-apprentices very soon began to feel it degrading to them to work with me. They began to **put on airs**, and talk about the "niggers" taking the country, saying we all ought to be killed; and, being encouraged by the journeymen, they commenced making my condition as hard as they could, by hectoring me around, and sometimes striking me. I, of course, kept the vow I

....

impropriety in it problem with that
knocked off stopped working
discharge fire; let go of
put on airs act like they were better than black men

made after the fight with Mr. Covey, and struck back again, regardless of consequences; and while I kept them from combining, I succeeded very well; for I could whip all of them, taking them separately. They, however, at length **combined, and came upon** me, armed with sticks, stones, and heavy **handspikes**. One came in front with a half brick. There was one at each side of me, and one behind me. While I was attending to those in front, and on either side, the one behind ran up with the handspike, and struck me a heavy blow upon the head. It stunned me. I fell, and with this they all ran upon me, and fell to beating me with their fists. I let them continue for a while, as I gathered strength. In an instant, I **gave a sudden surge**, and rose to my hands and knees. Just as I did that, one of them gave me, with his heavy boot, a powerful kick in the left eye. My eyeball seemed to have burst. When they saw my eye closed, and badly swollen, they left me. With this I seized the handspike, and for a time pursued them. But here the carpenters interfered, and I thought I might as well give it up. It was impossible to **stand my hand** against so many. All this took place in sight of not less

....

combined, and came upon joined, and attacked

handspikes metal bars

gave a sudden surge had a lot of energy

stand my hand fight alone

than fifty white ship-carpenters, and not one interposed a friendly word; but some cried, "Kill the damned nigger! Kill him! kill him! He struck a white person." I found my only chance for life was in flight. I succeeded in getting away without an additional blow, and barely so; for to strike a white man is death by **Lynch law,**— and that was the law in Mr. Gardner's shipyard; nor is there much of any other out of Mr. Gardner's shipyard.

I went directly home, and told the story of my wrongs to Master Hugh; and I am happy to say of him, **irreligious** as he was, his conduct was heavenly, compared with that of his brother Thomas under similar circumstances. He listened attentively to my narration of the circumstances leading to the savage outrage, and gave many proofs of his strong **indignation at** it. The heart of my once overkind mistress was again melted into pity. My puffed-out eye and blood-covered face moved her to tears. She took a chair by me, washed the blood from my face, and, with a mother's tenderness, bound up my head, covering the wounded eye with a lean piece of fresh beef. It was almost compensation for my suffering to witness, once more, a **manifestation** of

....

Lynch law hanging
irreligious mean
indignation at disagreement with
manifestation show

kindness from my once affectionate old mistress. Master Hugh was very much enraged. He gave expression to his feelings by **pouring out curses upon the heads of those** who did the deed. As soon as I got a little better from my bruises, he took me with him to Esquire Watson's, on Bond Street, to see what could be done about the matter. Mr. Watson inquired who saw the **assault committed**. Master Hugh told him it was done in Mr. Gardner's shipyard at midday, where there were a large company of men at work. "As to that," he said, "the deed was done, and there was no question as to who did it." His answer was, he could do nothing in the case, unless some white man would come forward and testify. He could issue no warrant on my word. If I had been killed in the presence of a thousand colored people, their testimony combined would have been insufficient to have arrested one of the murderers. Master Hugh, for once, was compelled to say **this state of things was too bad**. Of course, it was impossible to get any white man to volunteer his testimony in my behalf, and against the white young men. Even those who may have sympathized with me were not prepared

....

pouring out curses upon the heads of those swearing at the men

assault committed attack against me

this state of things was too bad that he felt sorry for my difficult situation

to do this. It required a degree of courage unknown to them to do so; for just at that time, the slightest manifestation of humanity toward a colored person was denounced as abolitionism, and that name **subjected its bearer to frightful liabilities**. The watchwords of the bloody-minded in that region, and in those days, were, "Damn the abolitionists!" and "Damn the niggers!" There was nothing done, and probably nothing would have been done if I had been killed. Such was, and such remains, the state of things in the Christian city of Baltimore.

Master Hugh, finding he could get no **redress**, refused to let me go back again to Mr. Gardner. He kept me himself, and his wife dressed my wound till I was again restored to health. He then took me into the shipyard of which he was foreman, in the employment of Mr. Walter Price. There I was immediately set to calking, and very soon learned the art of using my **mallet and irons**. In the course of one year from the time I left Mr. Gardner's, I was able to command the highest wages given to the most experienced calkers. I was now of some importance to my master. I was

....

subjected its bearer to frightful liabilities put the person at risk

redress justice for the attack on me

mallet and irons tools

bringing him from six to seven dollars per week. I sometimes brought him nine dollars per week: my wages were a dollar and a half a day. After learning how to calk, I sought my own employment, made my own contracts, and collected the money which I earned. My pathway became much more smooth than before; my condition was now much more comfortable. When I could get no calking to do, I did nothing. During these leisure times, those old notions about freedom would come to me again. When in Mr. Gardner's employment, I was **kept in such a perpetual whirl of excitement**, I could think of nothing, scarcely, but my life; and in thinking of my life, I almost forgot my liberty. I have observed this in my experience of slavery—that whenever my condition was improved, instead of its increasing my contentment, it only increased my desire to be free, and set me to thinking of plans to gain my freedom. I have found that, to make a contented slave, it is necessary to make a thoughtless one. It is necessary to darken his moral and mental vision, and, as far as possible, to **annihilate the power of reason**. He must be able to **detect no inconsistencies** in slavery; he

....

kept in such a perpetual whirl of excitement always so busy

annihilate the power of reason end his ability to think for himself

detect no inconsistencies see no wrong

must be made to feel that slavery is right; and he can be brought to that only when he ceases to be a man.

I was now getting, as I have said, one dollar and fifty cents per day. I **contracted for it**; I earned it; it was paid to me; it was rightfully my own; yet, upon each returning Saturday night, I was compelled to deliver every cent of that money to Master Hugh. And why? Not because he earned it—not because he had any hand in earning it—not because I owed it to him—nor because he possessed the slightest shadow of a right to it; but solely because he had the power to **compel me to** give it up. **The right of the grim-visaged pirate upon the high seas is exactly the same.**

....

contracted for it found the jobs

compel me to make me

The right of the grim-visaged pirate upon the high seas is exactly the same. He was like a pirate or a thief.

BEFORE YOU MOVE ON...

1. **Inference** Reread pages 109–110. Why would a fellow slave betray Frederick and the other slaves?

2. **Conclusions** Reread pages 122–124. How did the attack and Frederick's new employment affect him?

LOOK AHEAD Read Chapter 11 to see if Frederick will become a free man.

CHAPTER XI

I now come to that part of my life during which I planned, and finally succeeded in making, my escape from slavery. But before narrating any of the peculiar circumstances, I think I should make known my intention not to state all the facts connected with the transaction. My reasons for pursuing this course may be understood from the following: First, were I to give a **minute statement** of all the facts, it is not only possible, but quite probable, that **others would thereby be involved in the most embarrassing difficulties**. Secondly, such a statement would most undoubtedly **induce greater vigilance** on the part of slaveholders than has existed before among them; which would, of course, be the means of guarding a door whereby some dear brother bondman might escape his galling chains. I deeply regret the necessity that impels me to suppress anything of importance connected with my experience in slavery. It would afford me great pleasure indeed, as

----

minute statement very detailed description

others would thereby be involved in the most embarrassing difficulties those who helped me might get in trouble

induce greater vigilance cause more watching

well as materially add to the interest of my narrative, if I were at liberty to gratify a curiosity, which I know exists in the minds of many, by an accurate statement of all the facts pertaining to my most fortunate escape. But I must **deprive myself of this pleasure**, and deprive the curious people of the gratification which such a statement would afford. I would allow myself to **suffer under the greatest imputations** which evil-minded men might suggest, rather than **exculpate myself**, and thereby run the hazard of closing the slightest avenue by which a brother slave might clear himself of the chains and fetters of slavery.

In the early part of the year 1838, I became quite restless. I could see no reason why I should, at the end of each week, pour the reward of my toil into the purse of my master. When I carried to him my weekly wages, he would, after counting the money, look me in the face with a robber-like fierceness, and ask, "Is this all?" He was satisfied with nothing less than the last cent. He would, however, when I made him six dollars, sometimes give me six cents, to encourage me. It had the opposite effect. I regarded it as a sort of admission of

....

deprive myself of this pleasure not give myself the satisfaction of telling all the details

suffer under the greatest imputations be accused of terrible wrongs

exculpate myself clear myself of guilt

my right to the whole. The fact that he gave me any part of my wages was proof, to my mind, that he believed me entitled to the whole of them. I always felt worse for having received anything; for I feared that the giving me a few cents would ease his conscience, and make him feel himself to be a pretty honorable sort of robber. My discontent grew. I was always on the look-out for means of escape; and, finding no direct means, I determined to try to **hire my time**, with a view of getting money with which to make my escape. In the spring of 1838, when Master Thomas came to Baltimore to purchase his spring goods, I got an opportunity, and applied to him to allow me to hire my time. He unhesitatingly refused my request, and told me this was another stratagem by which to escape. He told me I could go nowhere but that he could get me; and that, in the event of my running away, he should spare no pains in his efforts to catch me. He **exhorted me to content myself**, and be obedient. He told me, if I wanted to be happy, I must lay out no plans for the future. He said, if I behaved myself properly, he would take care of me. Indeed, he advised me to **complete thoughtlessness of** the future, and

....

hire my time work on my own
exhorted me to content myself told me to be satisfied
complete thoughtlessness of not think about

taught me to depend solely upon him for happiness. He seemed to see **fully the pressing necessity of setting aside** my intellectual nature, so I would be content in slavery. But in spite of him, and even in spite of myself, I continued to think, and to think about the injustice of my enslavement, and the means of escape.

About two months after this, I applied to Master Hugh for the privilege of hiring my time. He was not acquainted with the fact that I had applied to Master Thomas and had been refused. He, too, at first, seemed disposed to refuse; but, after some reflection, he granted me the privilege, and proposed the following terms: I was to be allowed all my time, make all contracts with those for whom I worked, and find my own employment; and, in return for this liberty, I was to pay him three dollars at the end of each week; **find myself in calking tools, and in board and clothing**. My board was two dollars and a half per week. This, with the wear and tear of clothing and calking tools, made my regular expenses about six dollars per week. This amount I was compelled to make up, or relinquish the privilege of hiring my time. Rain

....

fully the pressing necessity of setting aside that he should not encourage

find myself in calking tools, and in board and clothing pay for my own tools, shelter, and clothes

or shine, work or no work, at the end of each week the money must be forthcoming, or I must give up my privilege. This arrangement, it will be perceived, was decidedly in my master's favor. It relieved him of all need of looking after me. His money was sure. He received all the benefits of slaveholding without its evils; while I endured all the evils of a slave, and suffered all the care and anxiety of a free man. I found it a hard bargain. But, hard as it was, I thought it better than the old mode of getting along. It was a step towards freedom to be allowed to **bear** the responsibilities of a free man, and I was determined to hold on **upon it**. I bent myself to the work of making money. I was ready to work at night as well as day, and by **the most untiring perseverance and industry**, I made enough to meet my expenses, and **lay up** a little money every week. I went on thus from May until August. Master Hugh then refused to allow me to hire my time longer. The ground for his refusal was a failure on my part, one Saturday night, to pay him for my week's time. I failed to pay on time because I was attending a camp meeting about ten miles from Baltimore. During the week, I had

....

bear have some of
upon it to these feelings of freedom
the most untiring perseverance and industry working hard
lay up save

entered into an engagement with a number of young friends to start from Baltimore to the campground early Saturday evening; and being **detained** by my employer, I was unable to get down to Master Hugh's without disappointing the company. I knew that Master Hugh was in no special need of the money that night. I therefore decided to go to camp meeting, and upon my return pay him the three dollars. I **staid** at the camp meeting one day longer than I intended when I left. But as soon as I returned, I called upon him to pay him what he considered his due. I found him very angry; he could **scarce restrain his wrath**. He said he had a great mind to give me a severe whipping. He wished to know how I dared go out of the city without asking his permission. I told him I hired my time and while I paid him the price which he asked for it, I did not know that I was bound to ask him when and where I should go. This reply troubled him; and, after reflecting a few moments, he turned to me, and said I could no longer hire my time; that the next thing he should know of, I would be running away. Upon the same plea, he told me to bring my tools and clothing

....

detained made to stay

staid stayed

scarce restrain his wrath not hold back his anger

home **forthwith**. I did so; but instead of seeking work, as I had been accustomed to do previously to hiring my time, I spent the whole week without **the performance of a single stroke of work**. I did this **in retaliation**. Saturday night, he called upon me as usual for my week's wages. I told him I had no wages; I had done no work that week. Here we almost came to blows. He raved, and swore his determination to get hold of me. I did not allow myself a single word; but was resolved, if he laid the weight of his hand upon me, it should be blow for blow. He did not strike me, but told me that he would find me **in constant employment in future**. I thought the matter over during the next day, Sunday, and finally resolved upon the third day of September, as the day upon which I would make a second attempt to secure my freedom. I now had three weeks during which to prepare for my journey. Early on Monday morning, before Master Hugh had time to make any engagement for me, I went out and got employment of Mr. Butler, at his shipyard near the drawbridge, upon what is called the City Block, thus making it unnecessary for him to seek

....

forthwith from then on

the performance of a single stroke of work doing any work

in retaliation to make Master Hugh angry

in constant employment in future work in the future

employment for me. At the end of the week, I brought him between eight and nine dollars. He seemed very well pleased, and asked why I did not do the same the week before. He little knew what my plans were. My object in working steadily was to remove any suspicion **he might entertain of my intent** to run away; and in this I succeeded admirably. I suppose he thought I was never better satisfied with my condition than at the very time during which I was planning my escape. The second week passed, and again I carried him my full wages; and so well pleased was he, that he gave me twenty-five cents (quite a large sum for a slaveholder to give a slave) and bade me to make a good use of it. I told him I would.

Things went on without very smoothly indeed, but **within there was trouble**. It is impossible for me to describe my feelings as the time of my **contemplated start drew near**. I had a number of warm-hearted friends in Baltimore—friends that I loved almost as I did my life—and the thought of being separated from them forever was painful beyond expression. It is my opinion that thousands would escape from slavery, who

....

he might entertain of my intent Master Hugh might have of my idea

within there was trouble I felt upset

contemplated start drew near planned escape came closer

now remain, but for the strong **cords of affection** that bind them to their friends. The thought of leaving my friends was decidedly the most painful thought with which I had to contend. The love of them was my **tender point, and shook my decision** more than anything else. Besides the pain of separation, the dread and apprehension of a failure exceeded what I had experienced at my first attempt. **The appalling defeat I then sustained returned to torment me.** I felt assured that, if I failed in this attempt, my case would be a hopeless one—it would seal my fate as a slave forever. I could not hope to get off with anything less than the severest punishment, and being placed beyond the means of escape. It required no very vivid imagination to depict the most frightful scenes through which I should have to pass, in case I failed. I constantly faced the wretchedness of slavery, and the blessedness of freedom. It was life and death with me. But I remained firm, and, according to my resolution, on the third day of September, 1838, I left my chains, and succeeded in reaching New York without the slightest interruption of any kind. How I did so—what means I adopted—

....

cords of affection feelings

tender point, and shook my decision weakness, and it made me question what I was doing

The appalling defeat I then sustained returned to torment me. Thoughts of my last failed escape bothered me.

what direction I travelled, and **by what mode of conveyance**—I must leave unexplained, for the reasons I mentioned before.

I have been frequently asked how I felt when I found myself in a **free State**. I have never been able to answer the question with any satisfaction to myself. It was a moment of the highest excitement I ever experienced. I suppose I felt as one may imagine the **unarmed mariner** to feel when he is rescued by a friendly man-of-war from the pursuit of a pirate. In writing to a dear friend, immediately after my arrival at New York, I said I felt like one who had escaped a den of hungry lions. This state of mind, however, very soon subsided; and I was again seized with a feeling of great insecurity and loneliness. I was yet liable to be taken back, and subjected to all the tortures of slavery. This in itself was enough to **damp the ardor of** my enthusiasm. But the loneliness overcame me. There I was in the midst of thousands, and yet a perfect stranger; without home and without friends, in the midst of thousands of my own brethren—children of a common Father, and yet I dared not to unfold to any one of them my sad condition.

....

by what mode of conveyance how I got there
free State state where slavery was not legal
unarmed mariner sailor with no weapon
damp the ardor of lessen

I was afraid to speak to anyone for fear of speaking to the wrong one, and thereby falling into the hands of money-loving kidnappers, whose business it was to lie in wait for the **panting fugitive**, as the ferocious beasts of the forest lie in wait for their prey. The motto which I adopted when I escaped from slavery was this— "Trust no man!" I saw in every white man an enemy, and in almost every colored man cause for distrust. It was a most painful situation; and, to understand it, one must experience it, or imagine himself in similar circumstances.

Thank Heaven, I remained but a short time in this distressed situation. I was relieved from it by the humane hand of MR. DAVID RUGGLES, whose vigilance, kindness, and perseverance, I shall never forget. I am glad of an opportunity to express, as far as words can, the love and gratitude I bear him. Mr. Ruggles is now afflicted with blindness, and is himself in need of the same kind **offices which he was once so forward in the performance of toward others**. I had been in New York but a few days, when Mr. Ruggles sought me out, and very kindly took me to his boardinghouse

....

panting fugitive nervous and exhausted runaway

offices which he was once so forward in the performance of toward others of help he gave to others

at the corner of Church and Lespenard Streets.
Mr. Ruggles was then very deeply engaged in the
memorable *Darg* case, as well as attending to a number
of other fugitive slaves, devising ways and means for
their successful escape; and, though watched and
hemmed in on almost every side, he seemed to be
more than a match for his enemies.

Very soon after I went to Mr. Ruggles, he wished to
know where I wanted to go; as he deemed it unsafe for
me to remain in New York. I told him I was a calker,
and should like to go where I could get work. I thought
of going to Canada; but he decided against it, and in
favor of my going to New Bedford, thinking I should
be able to get work there at my trade. At this time,
Anna, (she was free) my intended wife, **came on**; for I
wrote to her immediately after my arrival at New York
**(notwithstanding my homeless, houseless, and
helpless condition)** informing her of my successful
flight, and wishing her to come on forthwith. In a
few days after her arrival, Mr. Ruggles called in the
Reverend J. W. C. Pennington, who, in the presence
of Mr. Ruggles, Mrs. Michaels, and two or three

....

hemmed in trapped

came on came to be with me

**(notwithstanding my homeless, houseless, and
helpless condition)** (even though I did not have much)

others, performed the marriage ceremony, and gave us a certificate, of which the following is an exact copy—

This may certify, that I joined together in holy matrimony Frederick Johnson* and Anna Murray, as man and wife, in the presence of Mr. David Ruggles and Mrs. Michaels.

James W. C. Pennington
New York, Sept. 15, 1838.

Upon receiving this certificate, and a five-dollar bill from Mr. Ruggles, I **shouldered one part** of our baggage, and Anna took up the other, and we set out on the steamboat John W. Richmond for Newport, on our way to New Bedford. Mr. Ruggles gave me a letter to a Mr. Shaw in Newport, and told me, in case my money did not serve me to New Bedford, to stop in Newport and obtain further assistance; but upon our arrival at Newport, we were so anxious to get to a place of safety, that, **notwithstanding** we lacked the necessary money to pay our fare, we decided to take

*I had changed my name from Frederick *Bailey* to that of *Johnson*.

....

shouldered one part carried some
notwithstanding even though

seats in the stage, and promise to pay when we got to New Bedford. We were encouraged to do this by two excellent gentlemen, residents of New Bedford, whose names I afterward **ascertained to be** Joseph Ricketson and William C. Taber. They seemed at once to understand our circumstances, and gave us such assurance of their friendliness **as put us fully at ease** in their presence. It was good indeed to meet with such friends, at such a time. Upon reaching New Bedford, we were directed to the house of Mr. Nathan Johnson, by whom we were kindly **received, and hospitably provided for**. Both Mr. and Mrs. Johnson took a deep and lively interest in our welfare. They proved themselves quite worthy of the name of abolitionists. When the stagedriver found us unable to pay our fare, he held on upon our baggage as security for the debt. I had only to mention the fact to Mr. Johnson, and he immediately advanced the money.

We now began to feel a degree of safety, and to prepare ourselves for the duties and responsibilities of a life of freedom. On the morning after our arrival at New Bedford, while at the breakfast table, the question

....

ascertained to be learned were

as put us fully at ease that we felt completely comfortable

received, and hospitably provided for welcomed, and warmly taken care of

arose as to what name I should be called by. The name given me by my mother was "Frederick Augustus Washington Bailey." I, however, **had dispensed with** the two middle names long before I left Maryland so that I was generally known by the name of "Frederick Bailey." I started from Baltimore bearing the name of "Stanley." When I got to New York, I again changed my name to "Frederick Johnson," and thought that would be the last change. But when I got to New Bedford, I found it necessary again to change my name. The reason of this necessity was that there were so many Johnsons in New Bedford, so it was already quite difficult to **distinguish between them**. I gave Mr. Johnson the privilege of choosing me a name, but told him he must not take from me the name of "Frederick." I must hold on to that, to preserve a sense of my identity. Mr. Johnson had just been reading the "Lady of the Lake," and at once suggested that my name be "Douglass." From that time until now I have been called "Frederick Douglass"; and as I am more widely known by that name than by either of the others, I shall continue to use it as my own.

....

had dispensed with did not use
distinguish between them tell them apart

I was quite disappointed at the general appearance of things in New Bedford. The impression which I had **received respecting the character and condition of the people of the North, I found to be singularly erroneous**. I had very strangely supposed, while in slavery, that few of the comforts, and scarcely any of the luxuries, of life were enjoyed at the North, compared with what were enjoyed by the slaveholders of the South. I probably came to this conclusion from the fact that northern people owned no slaves. I supposed that they were about upon a level with the non-slaveholding population of the South. I knew *they* were exceedingly poor, and I had been accustomed to regard their poverty as the necessary consequence of their being non-slaveholders. I had somehow **imbibed the opinion** that, in the absence of slaves, there could be no wealth, and very little refinement. And upon coming to the North, I expected to meet with a rough, hard-handed, and uncultivated population, living in the most **Spartan-like simplicity**, knowing nothing of the ease, luxury, pomp, and grandeur of Southern slaveholders. Such being my conjectures, anyone

....

received respecting the character and condition of the people of the North, I found to be singularly erroneous about the people in the North was wrong

imbibed the opinion thought

Spartan-like simplicity bare and simple way

acquainted with the appearance of New Bedford may **very readily infer how palpably I must have seen** my mistake.

In the afternoon of the day when I reached New Bedford, I visited the wharves, to take a view of the shipping. Here I found myself surrounded with the strongest proofs of wealth. Lying at the wharves, and riding in the stream, I saw many ships of the finest model, in the best order, and of the largest size. Upon the right and left, I was **walled in by granite** warehouses of the widest dimensions, stowed to their utmost capacity with the necessaries and comforts of life. Added to this, almost everybody seemed to be at work, but noiselessly so, compared with what I had been accustomed to in Baltimore. There were no loud songs heard from those engaged in loading and unloading ships. I heard no deep oaths or horrid curses on the laborer. I saw no whipping of men; but all seemed to go smoothly on. Every man appeared to understand his work, and went at it with a sober, yet cheerful earnestness, which **betokened the deep interest which he felt in** what he was doing, as well as a

....

very readily infer how palpably I must have seen guess how much I knew

walled in by granite surrounded by tall stone

betokened the deep interest which he felt in showed how much he liked

sense of his own dignity as a man. To me this looked exceedingly strange. From the wharves I strolled around and over the town, gazing with wonder and admiration at the splendid churches, beautiful dwellings, and finely-cultivated gardens; **evincing** an amount of wealth, comfort, taste, and refinement such as I had never seen in any part of slaveholding Maryland.

Everything looked clean, new, and beautiful. I saw few or no **dilapidated houses, with poverty-stricken inmates**; no half-naked children and barefooted women, such as I had been accustomed to see in Hillsborough, Easton, St. Michael's, and Baltimore. The people looked more able, stronger, healthier, and happier, than those of Maryland. I was for once made glad by a view of extreme wealth, without being saddened by seeing extreme poverty. But the most astonishing as well as the most interesting thing to me was the condition of the colored people, a great many of whom, like myself, had escaped **thither as a refuge from the hunters of men**. I found many, who had not been seven years out of their chains, living in finer houses, and evidently enjoying more of the comforts of life, than the average

....

evincing showing

dilapidated houses, with poverty-stricken inmates
worn-down houses, with poor families living inside

thither as a refuge from the hunters of men there to find
safety

of slaveholders in Maryland. I will venture to assert that my friend Mr. Nathan Johnson (of whom I can say with a grateful heart, "I was hungry, and he gave me meat; I was thirsty, and he gave me drink; I was a stranger, and he took me in") lived in a neater house; dined at a better table; took, paid for, and read, more newspapers; better understood the moral, religious, and political character of the nation—than nine-tenths of the slaveholders in Talbot County, Maryland. Yet Mr. Johnson was a working man. His hands were hardened by **toil**, and not his alone, but those also of Mrs. Johnson. I found the colored people much more **spirited** than I had supposed they would be. I found among them a determination to protect each other from the bloodthirsty kidnapper, **at all hazards**.

I found employment, the third day after my arrival, in **stowing a sloop with a load of oil**. It was new, dirty, and hard work for me; but I went at it with a glad heart and a willing hand. I was now my own master. It was a happy moment, the rapture of which can be understood only by those who have been slaves. It was the first work, the reward of which was to be entirely my own.

....

toil hard work

spirited full of life

at all hazards no matter what

stowing a sloop with a load of oil putting oil onto ships

There was no Master Hugh standing ready, the moment I earned the money, to rob me of it. I worked that day with a pleasure I had never before experienced. I was at work for myself and newly-married wife. It was to me the starting-point of a new existence. When I got through with that job, I went in pursuit of a job of calking; but such was the strength of **prejudice against color**, among the white calkers, that they refused to work with me, and of course I could get no employment. (I am told that colored persons can now get employment at calking in New Bedford—a result of anti-slavery effort.) Finding my trade of no immediate benefit, I **threw off my calking habiliments**, and prepared myself to do any kind of work I could get to do. Mr. Johnson kindly let me have his woodhorse and saw, and I very soon found myself a plenty of work. There was no work too hard—none too dirty. I was ready to saw wood, shovel coal, carry wood, sweep the chimney, or roll oil casks—all of which I did.

In about four months after I went to New Bedford, there came a young man to me, and inquired if I **did not wish to take the "Liberator."** I told him I

....

prejudice against color racism

threw off my calking habiliments got rid of my tools

did not wish to take the "Liberator" wanted to buy an antislavery newspaper did; but, just having made my escape from slavery, I remarked that I was unable to pay for it then. I, however, finally became a subscriber to it. The paper came, and I read it from week to week with such feelings as it would be quite idle for me to attempt to describe. The paper became my meat and my drink. **My soul was set all on fire.** Its sympathy for **my brethren in bonds**—its **scathing denunciations** of slaveholders—its faithful exposures of slavery—and its powerful attacks upon the **upholders of the institution**—sent a thrill of joy through my soul, such as I had never felt before!

I had not long been a reader of the "Liberator," before I got a pretty correct idea of the principles, measures, and spirit of the anti-slavery reform. I embraced the cause. I could do little to help the cause; but what I could, I did with a joyful heart, and never felt happier than when in an anti-slavery meeting. I seldom had much to say at the meetings, because what I wanted to say was said so much better by others. But, while attending an anti-slavery convention at Nantucket, on the 11th of August, 1841, I felt strongly moved to speak, and was at the same time much urged to do so by Mr.

My soul was set all on fire. I was excited to read the paper.
my brethren in bonds people still in slavery
scathing denunciations strong disapproval
upholders of the institution people who supported slavery

William C. Coffin, a gentleman who had heard me speak in the colored people's meeting at New Bedford. **It was a severe cross, and I took it up reluctantly.** The truth was, I felt myself a slave, and the idea of speaking to white people weighed me down. I spoke but a few moments, when I felt a degree of freedom, and said what I desired with considerable ease. From that time until now, I have been **engaged in pleading the cause of my brethren**—with what success, and with what devotion, I leave those **acquainted with my labors** to decide.

....

It was a severe cross, and I took it up reluctantly. Speaking in front of white people was hard for me, and so I was not sure about doing it.

engaged in pleading the cause of my brethren speaking to many people against the idea of slavery

acquainted with my labors who know my work

BEFORE YOU MOVE ON...

1. **Author's Purpose** Frederick Douglass was once a slave. How did that affect the details he shared about his escape?

2. **Paraphrase** On page 146, Frederick says the *Liberator* was "my meat and my drink." Explain this in your own words.